CANOE ROUTES OF ONTARIO

Published by
Parks and Recreational Areas Branch
in cooperation with McClelland and Stewart

 Ministry of
Natural
Resources
Ontario

Hon. James A.C. Auld
Minister

W.T. Foster
Deputy Minister

© 1981 Ontario Ministry of Natural Resources
Queen's Park, Toronto

No part of this publication may be reproduced in
any form or by any means without permission in
writing from the Ontario Ministry of Natural Resources.

Ontario Ministry of Natural Resources Publication No. 5835/1981

Canadian Cataloguing in Publication Data
Main entry under title:
Canoe routes of Ontario
ISBN 0-7710-6067-X
1. Canoes and canoeing–Ontario. I. Ontario. Ministry of Natural
Resources.
GV776.15.05C36   797.1'22'09713   C81-094262-3

The Canadian Publishers
McClelland and Stewart Limited
25 Hollinger Road
Toronto M4B 3G2

Photo credits
Archives of Ontario: 10, 12, 22
Bruce Litteljohn: cover, 1, 4, 20
George Luste: 3, 7, 8, 13, 16, 21, 23, 24, 25, 27
Ministry of Natural Resources: title page, 2, 5, 6, 9, 11, 14, 15, 17, 18, 19, 26, 28

Printed and bound in Canada

Contents

Acknowledgements

The following people were involved in the preparation of *Canoe Routes of Ontario*. Mark Garscadden, concept and project direction; John Bemrose, text; Cathleen Hoskins, editor; Douglas Champion and Marjan Medved, design and production. The project would not have been possible without the full-hearted cooperation of Ministry of Natural Resources staff at regional and district offices throughout the province. In this regard special thanks are extended to Felix Barbetti, Dan Brunette, Fream Brown, John Featherstone, Tom Linklater, Craig MacDonald, Gerry O'Reilly and Barry Radford

Preface

Canoe Routes of Ontario is your key to one of the foremost canoeing regions in the world. In addition to being the most exhaustive compendium of canoe route information in the province, *Canoe Routes of Ontario* includes an unrivalled bibliography of source materials and an important essay on the geography of canoeing in Ontario. It also contains sections on safety and the new ethic of low-impact camping.

More and more people are discovering the joys of canoeing in Ontario. Its 400 000 lakes and countless kilometres of rivers offer something to meet the taste and skill of everyone, from families looking for a day of easy paddling to seasoned trippers with a preference for the isolation and challenge of the far North.

The province's offerings do not stop with its waterways. Vast forests shelter an abundance of animal life, from the shy and powerful moose to the inquisitive chipmunk. Over 270 species of birds nest here every year. The fishing is legendary, and the memory of pickerel fillets sizzling in the pan has enlivened the winter doldrums for more than one canoeist. The landscapes range from the gently pastoral to the ruggedly picturesque. No one who has paddled through southern Ontario farm lands in autumn or gazed up at the white quartzite hills of Killarney will soon forget them.

There is history here too, much of it of particular interest to the canoeist, for this was the part of the world that gave birth to the open canoe. For thousands of years Canada's waterways were the main transportation routes of her native peoples. Following their example, generations of explorers, fur traders, prospectors, settlers and fire rangers used the canoe to penetrate the forests of the interior. The canoeist who follows in their wake, who walks the same portage trails and camps by the same lakes and rivers, touches this country's past in a very immediate way.

Yet the greatest attraction for the canoeist is the activity itself, for it is an escape from the hurry and anxieties of urban life and a chance to refurbish body and spirit in the rhythm of the paddle.

Introduction

Canoe Routes of Ontario describes well over a hundred canoe routes across the province. It gives their locations, lengths, degrees of difficulty and some information about their history and the landscapes they flow through. It tells what game fish are available and what special conditions you may meet, such as low water late in the season. In short, *Canoe Routes of Ontario* gives enough information to allow you to select a route. Your choice made, you must then write to the appropriate district office of the Ministry of Natural Resources or Conservation Authority, which will send you a brochure or annotated map describing the route in enough detail to enable you to travel it.

A warning then: This book is not a navigational guide. It is a guide to the detailed literature written by field staff of the Ministry of Natural Resources and the Conservation Authorities. This literature is usually free of charge, and it gives the locations of access roads, rapids, portages and, very often, campsites. In most cases it also gives the identification numbers of the topographic maps without which no route should ever be travelled. (The ordering of topographic maps is described on page 107.)

The district offices of the Ministry of Natural Resources and the Conservation Authorities try to maintain the routes described in this book by keeping portages and campsites cleared. However, you must be prepared for the unexpected: Trees may blow down over portages in the intervals between maintenance patrols, and some campsites may be closed because they have been over-used. These will be minor inconveniences, of course, to the avid canoeist.

Geography of Canoeing in Ontario

There is astonishing natural diversity in Ontario. In the far North subarctic conditions prevail, and polar bears roam the windswept coasts of Hudson and James Bays. Yet the milder South nourishes the Kentucky coffee tree, common to the more temperate forests of the eastern United States. There is great variety in the landscape as well, from the flat, prosperous farm land of the south-western Ontario peninsula to the fortress-like cliffs that abut the Lake Superior shore. The canoeist would do well to master the basics of Ontario's geography. Such knowledge will not only help him to prepare adequately for his trip, but will also increase his enjoyment of what he sees.

The Canadian Shield

Anyone travelling from southern into northern Ontario is soon struck by an extraordinary transformation of the landscape. The rolling farm lands of the South give way to dense forests, massive outcrops of rock and a seem-ingly endless number of lakes and rivers. This is Shield country, a rugged but beautiful land that has made a deep impression on Canada's history and imagination. It has drawn traders hungry for its furs and lumbermen and prospectors eager to exploit its great natural wealth. It has frustrated railwaymen struggling to lay track across its gorges and swamps and has attracted cottagers and fishermen with its unspoiled waters. Yet through all this the Shield has remained sparsely settled. Much of it is uncrossed by highways, and the few mining and pulp and paper towns are but specks on its vastness. This starkly beautiful land has been celebrated by the artists of the Group of Seven, who found inspiration here for a new kind of landscape painting. Their canvases brim with the vivid autumn colours and the dramatic contrasts between forest and sky that are typical of Shield country. Even their titles evoke the Shield: *Algoma Country, Jack Pine, Northern River.*

Shield country takes its name from the Canadian Shield, a huge band of bedrock that sweeps across much of Canada, from the arctic seas in the northwest to Labrador in the east. (See figure 2.) Its rocks are frequently exposed and represent the roots of ancient mountain ranges that were built up over billions of years and then gradually

worn away by running water and wind. Over the last few million years several glaciers have spread down from the north, eroding the Shield's surface, picking up soil and rocks and depositing them as far south as southern Ontario and the northern United States. The most recent of the glacial periods ended but a few thousand years ago. In some places the ice has left the Shield bedrock covered with soils and rocks of every description; in others it has scraped the rock bare. Sometimes this exposed rock is marked with scratches and long parallel grooves created by sharp rocks embedded in the underside of the advancing ice.

Long periods of upheaval and erosion have left the Shield landscape broken with cliffs, gorges, valleys and hills, creating a multitude of nesting places for water. Anyone who has looked at a detailed map of the region or flown above it can attest to its bewildering mazes of lakes and rivers. The uneven bedrock ensures that these waterways never flow smoothly for long: Sooner or later, planes of flat water always end in rapids or falls where the water plunges to the next level. The canoeist may curse this "terraced" effect as he shoulders his gear for the hike around the rapids, but he should remember that the open canoe was invented by the Indians to meet just these conditions. Light and manageable, it can be guided through white water or portaged by a single man. The first European explorers were skeptical of this fragile craft, but they soon became converts. The open canoe remained the major vehicle of exploration for much of Canada until the advent of the airplane.

The rocks of the Shield contain tremendous mineral wealth, and over the last century mining towns have sprung up across the northland with the discovery of nickel and copper at Sudbury, iron in the Atikokan and Wawa areas, silver and cobalt at Cobalt, gold at Porcu-pine, Kirkland Lake and Red Lake, uranium at Elliot Lake, and silver, gold, lead and zinc at Timmins. But not every mine came up to expectations. Sometimes the canoeist will come across clearings where ruined buildings and rusted machines are slowly succumbing to the undergrowth, reminders of thousands of hours of work and many dead hopes.

2 *Over Quetico Provincial Park. Shield country's thousands of lakes and rivers offer endless canoeing possibilities.*

3 *Not all portages are as level—or as dry—as this one.*

Most of Ontario's Shield country is covered with the boreal forest. (See figure 1.) This is the "evergreen" forest of popular imagination. It is usually dominated by a handful of coniferous species, mainly black and white spruce, jack pine and balsam fir. These trees are cold-tolerant and so have a competitive edge over the broadleaved species, which are more vulnerable to the severe northern winters. The boreal species have other advantages. The jack pine, for example, is particularly well adapted for survival in the fires that frequently ravage the boreal forest. Though the fire consumes

the parent tree, its heat dries and opens the cones. The fire also burns away the organic layers of the soil and exposes the mineral soil in which the jack pine seeds are especially adapted to take root.

South of the boreal forest a more moderate climate has promoted the growth of broadleaves, such as red and sugar maple, yellow birch, red oak, basswood, beech and butternut, as well as white hemlock, red and white pine and an admixture of species from the boreal forest. This Great Lakes–St. Lawrence forest extends beyond the

2

3

southern boundaries of the Shield and well into southern Ontario. (See figure 1.)

It should be emphasized that the division of the Shield's forests into two regions hardly does justice to the variations in forest cover found from one locale to another. The canoeist can enrich his trip by picking out these variations and by trying to understand how local climate, topography and soil cover have led to the predominance of certain species. On the Sand River in Lake Superior Provincial Park, for example, he will notice that the riverbanks are covered with black spruce and with willow and alder thickets. These are hardy, moisture-loving trees capable of doing well in the water-retaining clays of the cool, shady river valley. But if the canoeist climbs to the tops of the nearby Algoma Hills, he will find himself in groves of sugar maple. These trees flourish in the thin, dry soils and plentiful sunlight of the summits. In autumn they turn a vivid crimson, giving the Algoma Hills their famous "red caps".

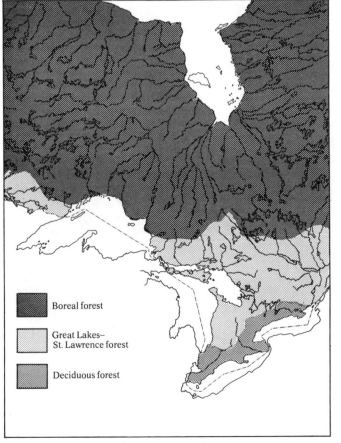

Boreal forest

Great Lakes–
St. Lawrence forest

Deciduous forest

Fig. 1 Forest Regions of Ontario (*Modified from J. Rowe*)

The red and white pine of the Great Lakes–St. Lawrence forest fed a booming lumber industry in the nineteenth and early twentieth centuries. The tall, straight trunks of these magnificent trees were ideal for the manufacture of ships' masts and timbers and for the beams and planks used in general construction. In fact, a great part of the American Midwest was built with Canadian timber. The trunks were cut and trimmed in the winter, when the

4 *A camp in Shield country.*

5 *"Voyageurs" paddle a* canot de maître *in this historical re-enactment. Lake Superior's Sleeping Giant lies in the background.*

snow made it easy to haul them by sledge to the riverbanks; after breakup they were floated down the rivers to the sawmills. Most of the biggest pine are gone today, but a few survive in the interior of Algonquin Park and on the shores of Lake Temagami. These trees tower above the surrounding forest and are so thick that two men cannot join hands around their bases.

Although the pineries themselves have largely vanished, evidence of the old logging days has not. Ring bolts, once used to anchor log booms, can still be found embedded

4

munks, squirrels and that nervy, bright-eyed bird, the whiskey jack, with his talent for nipping away with bits of food when the cook's not looking. Around the evening campfire it is common to hear the liquid call of a loon or whippoorwill drift in across the dimming water. Evening is also the best time to try to howl up a wolf. (A word for the timid: In Ontario there has never been a recorded attack by a wolf on a human being.)

Another animal of the Shield, the beaver, provided the incentive for the exploration of much of Canada by

5

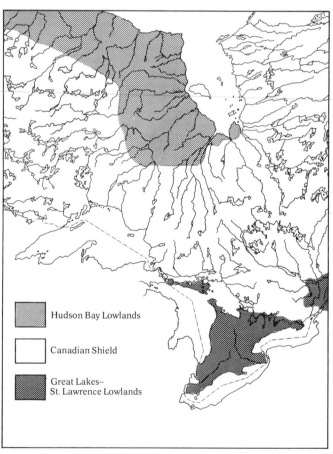

in the rock along many rivers. The canoeist may also run across the ruins of wooden chutes that were used to transport logs around falls and rapids where jams might occur. And if he looks carefully, he may find the remains of camps where lumberjacks once worked sixteen-hour days, ate prodigious quantities of flapjacks and salt pork, quarreled and played the fiddle.

Although lumbering is still carried out on the Shield, its importance is exceeded today by that of the pulp and paper industry, which cares not so much for the width of trunk as for the bulk of the total harvest. Trees of every size are taken, some by chainsaw, some by mechanical harvesters that cut and strip the trunks in a single operation. Before World War II most pulpwood was floated down the rivers to the mills, but now it is trucked. In towns such as Spanish, Dryden and Red Rock the wood is processed into the pulp from which newsprint and other paper products are produced. Canada is a world-leader in the export of pulp and newsprint.

A silently gliding canoe is an ideal spot from which to observe the wildlife of the Shield. The hopes of stealing up on a feeding moose rise more often than they are fulfilled, but such encounters *do* happen. The canoeist is more likely to stir up a flock of ducks or spot a slowly wheeling hawk or eagle or, perhaps, float close to a great blue heron before he crooks his long neck and flaps away. In camp it is the small creatures that appear: chip-

Hudson Bay Lowlands

Canadian Shield

Great Lakes– St. Lawrence Lowlands

Fig. 2 Physiographic Regions of Ontario (*Modified from H.S. Bostock*)

6 *Living things of the Shield: whiskey jack, white pines at sunset, moose, a water lily.*

Europeans, who from the 1600s to the mid 1800s sought its thick fur for the beaver felt hats then fashionable in Britain and on the Continent. The English and Scottish factors of the Hudson's Bay Company, the oldest chartered company in the world, built their first trading posts at the mouths of the great rivers flowing into Hudson and James Bays, then gradually extended their network of posts and supply routes inland. Later, Northwest Company voyageurs, paddling their twelve-metre *canots de maître* from Montreal to Lake Superior, began to draw large quantities of furs away to the south. Competition between the two companies grew fierce, ending only when the Hudson's Bay Company absorbed its rival in 1821. The canoeist who plies the Shield's waterways today is following in the wake of voyageurs, Métis and Orkneymen who bartered kettles, guns and trinkets for pelts, and whose ribald paddling songs echoed across the forests. The passage of the fur brigades has left little physical trace: here a worn stepping stone on a portage, there a mouldering cross beside a rapids. Yet many of the place names across the northland were bestowed by these early adventurers: *Grande Portage,* Baptism River, Fort Hope.

The waterways of the Shield open up any time from April to mid June, depending on latitude and local mitigating influences, such as proximity to the Great Lakes. Because of melting snow, spring waters are high, powerful and extremely cold: A dunking could easily prove fatal in a few minutes. Yet some of the best canoeing is to be found in this season, when rocky river bottoms are well sub-merged, blackflies and mosquitoes are kept down by late frosts, and the warm spring sun invigorates the spirit.

Summer days on the Shield are long and often hot. The nights are usually cool enough to sleep comfortably, though tents and mosquito netting are a must. Lake shallows generally become warm enough for swimmers to enjoy themselves for hours. Rain is always a possibility. Showers can come and go in an hour or stay for a week, especially in late August.

The levels of some rivers drop considerably over the summer, exposing rocks and making rapids difficult to run. In some cases passages are unnavigable. It is wise to check water levels at the appropriate Ministry of Natural Resources district office before setting out.

Frosts arrive by late August or early September. These have the twofold advantage of killing the bugs and turning the broadleaved trees yellow and orange and red. Snow may fall quite early, and the water grows rapidly colder as the November–December freeze-up approaches.

Finding a good campsite is rarely a problem on the Shield; an open space with a nice view can usually be found close to the water, often in a picturesque grove of mature trees. Points and islands are favourite places to pitch a tent, for a cross-breeze usually keeps bugs to a minimum.

The majority of routes in this book are on the Shield, and the canoeist who follows even a few of them will soon discover the diversity of the Shield's offerings. There are more landscapes waiting here, more lakes and rivers, than a lifetime of canoeing could exhaust.

7

8

The Hudson Bay Lowlands

Many rivers, such as the Albany, the Missinaibi and the Mattagami, originate on the Canadian Shield and descend in rapids, waterfalls and fast water onto a very different type of terrain. The rocky shores typical of so much of the Shield give way to high gravel and mud banks, and the rivers themselves broaden and straighten out as they flow toward the sea. The terraced effect encountered on Shield waterways disappears on this more level terrain, and rapids are less frequent.

The Hudson Bay Lowlands is a vast, flat, sodden plain abutting Hudson and James Bays. (See figure 2.) It is underlaid by sedimentary rocks, mainly limestones, dolomites and shales. These rocks are covered by sands and tills deposited by retreating glaciers, and by marine clay deposited by seas that covered the area in post-glacial periods. The rivers of the Lowlands have eroded deep channels into these glacial and marine deposits, creating the high riverbanks typical of the region. In some places rivers have cut into bedrock through this process

9 *Indian boatmen poling up rapids on the Abitibi River near the turn of the century.*

10 *The flat, sodden Hudson Bay Lowlands. In the background a river snakes between its levee forests.*

of "entrenchment"; where the water is shallow the canoeist may see bedrock shelves pass beneath the canoe.

The entrenchment of these rivers is being aided by a phenomenon known as isostatic rebound. The tremendous weight of the glaciers actually depressed the bedrock, rather in the way a rubber ball is depressed by squeezing. Now that the glaciers are gone, the bedrock is rebounding, creating an upward momentum that in combination with the downward erosion of the river helps the entrenchment process.

Isostatic rebound is shaping the Lowlands in yet another way. The area is extremely flat and slopes at an almost negligible gradient into Hudson and James Bays, creating very shallow coastal seas. As the land rebounds, more and more of it emerges from the water, with the result that the Lowlands is constantly growing in area.

Evidence of this process can be seen in the long, parallel ridges of slightly raised ground that cover much of the Lowlands. Each of these is a beach ridge, an ancient shoreline where waves heaped up sand, gravel and shells.

9

10

As the Bays retreated, these old shores were left high and dry. Today, the oldest of them are hundreds of kilometres from the sea.

The extreme flatness of the terrain, the moisture-holding quality of the marine clay and the presence of permafrost (a layer of the ground that never thaws out) have resulted in very poor drainage. Thus, the Lowlands is largely waterlogged, covered with bogs and fens where the forests of the Shield could never flourish. The fens are dominated by sedges, and in the bogs grow plants such as leather-leaf, pitcher plant, sundew, bog laurel and bog rosemary. On the higher, drier beach ridges are found heaths, such as Labrador tea, and other plants with arctic affinities, such as saxifrages and crowberry.

The high banks of the rivers (or levees) present a very different appearance. The better drainage and the shelter provided by the banks permits the growth of trees, such as black spruce and balsam poplar, as well as alder and willow thickets. These levee forests can grow quite thick,

11 *Low tide near the mouth of a Lowlands river.*

12 *Indians of northern Ontario constructing a birchbark canoe in the traditional manner around the turn of the century.*

13 *A campsite on a gravel bar of a Lowlands river. The forested levee rises in the background.*

giving the canoeist an impression of paddling down a heavily treed corridor. But beyond the levee these apparent forests soon peter out into the bleaker, wetter habitats (or muskeg) described above.

On the coasts and in the river estuaries are found saline and brackish marshes, where plants such as mare's tail form thick swards. These marshes provide a nesting ground for the vast flocks of snow and Canada geese that darken the northern flyways in spring and autumn.

lynx—in short, many of the species found on the Shield— do very well here, as do the arctic fox and several species of arctic birds, such as the ptarmigan. Sometimes beluga or white whales venture into the river estuaries, and some of the coastal areas are frequented by polar bears. The polar bear is especially dangerous and should never be approached. The most troublesome creature of the Lowlands, from man's point of view, is the mosquito, which swarms in clouds from the wetlands during the brief summer.

11

12

13

This is a harsh country, at least as far as man is concerned. Except for a few seasonal hunting camps, settlement has not expanded beyond the isolated communities founded by native people and Hudson's Bay Company factors at the mouths of several of the largest rivers. Yet moose, wolf, caribou, beaver, snowy owl,

Although most of these rivers are not technically so difficult as those on the Shield, they are dangerous because of their extreme isolation. There are other complicating factors. Poor drainage and the gooey marine clay of the banks can make good camping places hard to find; hip waders may be necessary on some portages. The dry period in late summer may lower some rivers, exposing boulders and gravel bars between which the canoeist must wade or zigzag endlessly. Navigation on river estuaries is often made difficult by strong winds off the Bays, by the tide and by mazes of channels and islands that can bewilder a canoeist for days. No canoeist should ever venture onto the open Bays without a guide, since conditions can be extremely treacherous.

The weather on the Lowlands is highly unstable. The canoeing season is short, lasting at best from late June to

14

mid September for those rivers north of the Albany. Although some days may be warm and sunny, rain and snow can strike anytime, and raingear and a change of cold-weather clothing are essential.

This is a region with a beauty all its own. It is isolated,

and its rivers flow for great distances. The canoeist can feel very small on one of these great waterways.

The Great Lakes–St. Lawrence Lowlands

The Great Lakes–St. Lawrence Lowlands is familiar to most of the people of Ontario, for most of them live there. The Lowlands is blanketed by farm lands, woodlots, roads, villages, towns and cities. The lay of the land is rather flat, though in some areas considerable local relief is afforded by hills and shallow valleys. There are few lakes in the Lowlands (though the Great Lakes of

15

Ontario, Erie and Huron are dramatic exceptions); but there are a fair number of canoeable rivers.

The proximity of these rivers to settlement is considered an advantage by many canoeists: by those, for example, who are learning the art of canoeing in their spare time, by those with children who do not want to expose them to the isolation and cold waters of the Shield and by those who prefer short day trips close to home. They are also attractive to those with a taste for historical sites and creature comforts provided by the occasional town or village. In fact, many of these rivers offer the best of both worlds: the nearness of civilization combined with the sense of isolation that can be experienced amid the forests that still cover many riverbanks.

The Great Lakes–St. Lawrence Lowlands is underlaid by sedimentary rocks, mainly limestones and dolomites. These rocks are covered with glacial drift (loose rocks, gravel, sand and clay deposited by glaciers) and are rarely exposed. The physiography of the Lowlands is very complex, and a look at the literature listed in Sources of Further Information under "Nature Guides" is highly recommended.

The rivers are good places from which to observe details of the geological history of the Lowlands. Take the Grand River for example. Near Elora it has cut deeply into the limestone bedrock, creating a deep gorge. Farther downstream the river flows past high bluffs composed of great thicknesses of glacial drift; in places eskers (sinuous, snake-like hills) can be seen on top of the bluffs. Near Paris the Grand flows over extensive gravel beds, which mark the presence of old glacial spillways (the channels where melt water laden with sand and gravel drained away from receding glaciers). Below Brantford the river broadens, becomes more sluggish and meanders in great curves. The terraced hills in the farm lands on either side of the river indicate former riverbanks. Like many Lowlands rivers, the Grand has a turbid look because of the

head. In other areas where the soil was sandy and well drained, oak plains sometimes flourished; mature oaks stood far apart, and grasses and wildflowers billowed in the open spaces.

The forests fell to the axes of the settler and the lumberman, and the woodlots that survived them have rarely reached the magnificence of their predecessors. However, the riverbank forests were always more tangled affairs, with undergrowth and trees of every height struggling for a place in the sun. And many of them are just as densely

16

soil and other materials it is constantly eroding, transporting and depositing in its dynamic shaping of the valley.

The forests that covered the Lowlands when the pioneers arrived and the remnants that survive today include the southern reaches of the Great Lakes–St. Lawrence forest and, south of this, a deciduous or broadleaved forest. (See figure 1.) This deciduous forest lies in the peninsula of southwestern Ontario and includes both broadleaves from the Great Lakes–St. Lawrence forest, such as sugar maple, white elm, basswood, butternut and white oak, and broadleaves from the Carolinian forest of the eastern United States, which have here reached the northern limit of their range. These include the tulip tree, the Kentucky coffee tree, sassafras, hickory, sycamore and black walnut.

In pioneer times these Lowlands forests were such that one could walk for kilometres in a cool, twilight world untroubled by undergrowth, for little sun made it through the dense canopy of leaves that started ten metres over-

overgrown today. A canoeist can be close to county roads, farms and towns and yet have all these screened from ear and eye.

Many of the river valleys abound in wildlife, from hawks, herons, cliff swallows, redwing blackbirds and numerous other birds to coyotes, foxes, deer, raccoons, skunks, chipmunks and squirrels. Nature is surprisingly productive in these parts, and more than one canoeist has known the irony of seeing more wild animals here than on the "wilds" of the Shield.

A few of the rivers offer good canoeing throughout the season. But many are canoeable only in spring and early summer, since later they shrink to mere trickles and make navigation extremely difficult. Sometimes, however, autumn rains augment their flow and permit canoeing late in the season. Many rivers do not freeze until January and are ice-free again in March.

It should be noted that many of the rivers of southern

Ontario flow past private property. Campsites are not always readily available. In the interests of good canoeist-landowner relations, it is wise to check beforehand for the location of public campgrounds. If these do not exist, you must obtain permission from property owners.

How to Choose a Route

Your choice of a route will be governed by many factors, including distance to the canoeing location, time available, your level of skill and your preference for lake or river travel and for a certain type of landscape.

Perhaps the best way to begin is to spread out the large map inserted into the book. You will be able to tell at a glance what routes lie within your travel range, their access points, configurations and approximate lengths. You will notice that individual routes are coloured blue and numbered. The routes are of two types. Linear routes begin and end at separate points; loop routes circle back to their starting places.

The map also contains twenty-one canoe areas, shaded in green and labelled from A to U. A canoe area contains such a dense concentration of routes, many of them interlocking, that it would be impossible to outline all of them on a map of this scale. Some of the best canoeing in the province is to be found within canoe areas.

When you find a route or area that interests you, use its number or letter to look up the corresponding description in this book. There is an index on page 110.

For your convenience the large inserted map has been divided into five sections (see key map, p. 21), making five smaller maps that are included at intervals throughout the book. Each map is followed by the descriptions of the routes and areas that appear on it.

Canoe Routes

1 The first line of each route description contains the number and the name of the route:

Route (68) Upper Mississagi River.

2 The second line indicates whether the route is principally a lake route, a river route or contains large elements of both:

Type Lake and river route.

When a route is described as a river route, this means that it is composed mainly (at least 85 per cent) of river travel; it may contain a small amount of lake travel. Similarly, a lake route may contain a small amount of river travel. The designations "lake and river route" or "river and lake route" signify large elements of both types of travel.

3 The third line of the description contains a difficulty rating for the route. This rating is broken down into four categories, each labelled A, B or C. A typical entry looks like this:

Rating A A C B.

River travel: The first category (the first A in the example) refers to the difficulty of river travel on the route. This is not a white water rating; it is assumed the canoeist will overcome rapids by either lining or portaging. The rivers were rated in May to early June, when water levels are still reasonably high. A few far northern rivers were rated in midsummer, the only time when they are warm enough to be canoed.

C is the easiest level. It means that
a) portages are easily recognized and easy to reach because of a slow current
b) river bottoms and shores are largely free of debris and other obstructions to canoe travel
c) there is a single, easily recognized channel for navigation.

B is the intermediate level. It means that
a) portages are usually easy to recognize, but the approaches to some may require manoeuvring in a moderate current
b) there may be sections of river bottom and shore where debris and obstructions require attention and manoeuvring
c) there may be sections with two or more channels, but the correct choice is generally easy to make.

A is the most difficult level. It means that
a) portages may be difficult to recognize, and a high degree of alertness is necessary since the approaches to some may require manoeuvring in a swift current
b) there may be many long sections of river bottom and shore where debris and obstructions require constant

attention and manoeuvring

c) there may be sections with a maze of channels and the correct choice may be difficult to make

d) there may be no portages on stretches of white water, and running, poling or lining will be required.

Lake travel: The second category (the second A in the example) refers to the difficulty of travel on open bodies of water on the route. These bodies will most often be lakes, though in some instances very wide rivers will react like lakes in the wind, making the same strenuous demands on the canoeist.

C is the easiest level. It means that

a) there are few if any safety problems

b) there are sheltered bodies of water where wind, although it may be stiff at times, does not generate high waves

c) landing spots or sheltered areas are numerous

d) canoeists are rarely, if ever, wind-bound.

B is the intermediate level. It means that

a) there are safety problems, but they can easily be avoided

b) there are bodies of water with exposed areas where the wind may generate waves high enough to swamp an open canoe

c) landing spots or sheltered areas are usually available

d) canoeists may be wind-bound for parts of some days or, on occasion, for day-long periods

e) weather and potentially exposed stretches are readily predictable.

A is the most difficult level. It means that

a) there are safety problems that are frequent and sometimes unavoidable

b) there are exposed bodies of water where the wind frequently generates waves high enough to swamp a canoe

c) landing spots and sheltered areas may be infrequent

d) canoeists may be wind-bound for a day or longer

e) the body of water may be subject to sudden changes of weather, such as fog and wind direction.

Portages: The third category (C in the example) refers to the difficulty of portages on the route. It is assumed that all portages will be taken.

C is the easiest level. It means that

a) the longest portage is less than one kilometre

b) portages present few impediments to travel and feature good footing on flat to gently rolling terrain

c) the most difficult day of travel will not involve portaging more than a total of 1.5 kilometres.

B is the intermediate level. It means that

a) the longest portage is between one and three kilometres

b) some portages may have steep sections or short stretches where extra effort is required and where footing may not be firm

c) the most difficult day of travel may involve portaging a total of 1.5 to 3.5 kilometres.

A is the most difficult level. It means that

a) the longest portage is greater than three kilometres

b) portages may be over rough terrain and have extended stretches where extra effort is required and where the footing may not be firm

c) the most difficult day of travel may involve portaging a total of more than 3.5 kilometres.

Remoteness: The fourth category (B in the example) refers to the remoteness of the route. Distance from civilization is a factor that increases the dangers of any canoe trip for the simple reason that help is far away. If weak or inexperienced people are included on a trip, the remoteness factor should be considered as more severe.

C is the easiest level. It means that time by land and/or water to the nearest assured source of help is half a day's travel or less from the most remote part of the route.

B is the intermediate level. It means that the nearest assured help is a full day's travel away.

A is the most difficult level. It means that help is more than a day's travel away, and sources where supplies can be obtained are spaced more than a week apart.

Finally, if a category is not relevant to a route, an n/a (not applicable) sign will be inserted instead of the usual letter.

4 The fourth line in the route description indicates the total length of the route and an approximate travelling time for a canoeist paddling at an average rate without stopovers:

Length 104 km / 5 days.

5 The fifth line gives the total number of portages, and after the slash it lists portages that are especially difficult because of length (i.e. one kilometre and longer) or other noteworthy conditions:

Portages 16 / 2 km, 3.5 km, 144 m (steep and slippery).

This means that there are 16 portages in all, two of which (2 km and 3.5 km) are quite long and one of which, though short (only 144 m), is steep and slippery and likely to be arduous.

6 The sixth line lists the main bodies of water on the route:

Main bodies of water Klotz and Flint Lakes, Flint River.

7 The next line gives the principal starting point (a town or lake or river) and the means of access (road and/or rail or, where it provides the only access, air):

Start Woebegone by road (Hwy 65) or rail (VIA).

8 The next line gives the principal finishing point, using the same method:

Finish Stone Head by rail (Ontario Northland).

If it is a loop or circular route, beginning and ending at the same place, only one name will be given:

Start/Finish Astonish Lake by road (off Hwy 4).

9 The next line, entitled Intermediate Access, indicates points at which the route is intersected by roads or railways. These points can be used as alternate beginning or end points. This book mentions only major intermediate access points; others may be indicated in the literature provided by the Ministry of Natural Resources or Conservation Authorities and on topographic maps. Not all routes will have intermediate access points.

10 The first paragraph of the descriptive text provides a general overview of the route, with note to scenic, natural and historical features that are specific to the route. The second paragraph concerns special travel advisories, such as seasonal low water difficulties.

11 Listed under Detailed Information is the name of the brochure, annotated map or information sheet that will give the canoeist more detailed information which, when combined with topographic maps, will provide sufficient directions for travel. Unless stated otherwise, this material is provided free of charge. When writing to the address given for the detailed information, always include the full name of the desired brochure or map.

Canoe Areas

1 Each canoe area has a letter, which refers to its position on the map. The first line in each area description gives the letter and the name of the canoe area.

2 The second line indicates whether the canoe area offers mainly (at least 85 per cent) lake or river travel or a combination of both. No canoe area contains purely lake travel, as lakes will always be joined by at least small rivers.

3 The third line indicates the number of routes within each area and the range of lengths in kilometres and days.

4 The fourth line lists the main bodies of water in the canoe area.

5 The fifth line gives the principal access points or describes them in a general way if they are numerous. The material listed in the Detailed Information section will contain more complete information on access points.

6 The descriptive text provides a thumbnail sketch of the canoe area—its history, topography, flora and fauna.

7 Under Detailed Information the available brochures and maps are listed with brief notes on what they contain. For some canoe areas pamphlets are available for individual routes. They are listed and described briefly. Unless stated otherwise, this material is provided free of charge. When writing to the address given for the detailed information, always include the full name of the desired brochure or map.

Note: Ministry of Natural Resources district offices and Conservation Authorities will not provide large quantities of free brochures in response to individual requests. However, priced publications may be ordered in large numbers.

Key Map

For your convenience the large inserted map has been divided into five
sections, making five smaller maps lettered A to E. These section maps
are found at intervals throughout the book. Each of the five section
maps is followed by the descriptions of the routes and areas that
appear on it. The page numbers of the section maps are as follows:
A, page 22; B, page 44; C, page 48; D, page 56; E, page 80.

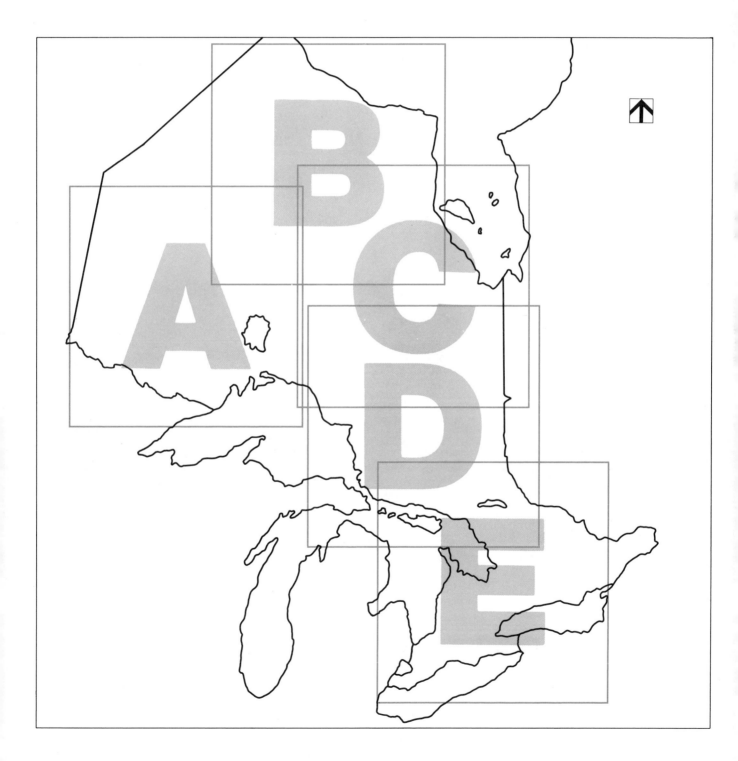

Route

1 Boundary Waters Fur Trade
2 Kaministikwia River Fur Trade
3 Kakagi Lake Loop
4 Vermilion Bay-Whitefish Bay Loop
5 Rushing River-Sioux Narrows Loop
6 Rushing River to Aulneau Peninsula Loop
7 Dogtooth-Kilvert-White Lake Loop
8 Kenora-Fort St. Charles Loop
9 Kenora-Cygnet Lake Loop
10 Blue Lake Loop
11 Upper Wabigoon-English River
12 Red Lake-Longlegged Lake Loop
13 Red Lake-Carroll Lake
14 Pakwash-Trout-Bruce Lake Loop

15 Sioux Lookout or Lake St. Joseph to Red Lake
16 Press Lake to Sioux Lookout
17 Savant Lake-Sioux Lookout Loop
18 Upper Albany River
19 Lake St. Joseph to Menako Lakes
20 Kawinogans-Bow-Otoskwin Loop
21 Gull River

Area

A Quetico Provincial Park
B Atikokan
C White Otter
D Fort Frances
(Continued opposite)

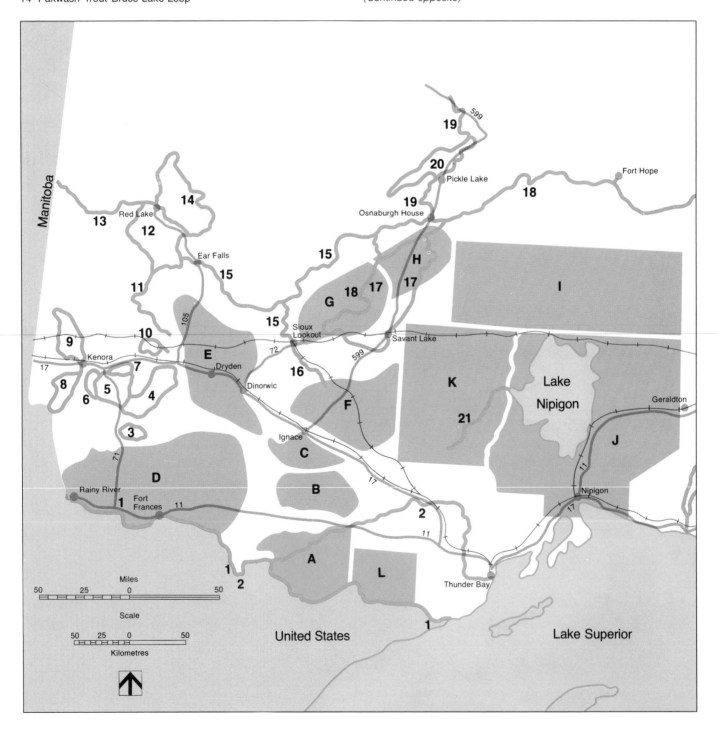

E   Dryden
F   Sandbar
G   Sioux Lookout
H   De Lesseps
I   Whitewater Lake-Ogoki Reservoir
J   Nipigon
K   Graham
L   Northern Light Lake

Route (1) Boundary Waters Fur Trade

Type River and lake route

Rating B B A B

Length 520 km / 20 to 30 days

Portages 43 / 13.6 km

Main bodies of water Pigeon River, Saganaga, Basswood and Rainy Lakes, Rainy River, Lake of the Woods

Start Pigeon River by road (Hwy 61, 7 km south of the Ontario-Minnesota border)

Finish Rainy River by road (Hwy 11)

Intermediate access Fort Frances by road (Hwy 11), Quetico Provincial Park and Northern Light Lake by water

Travelled for centuries by Indians, this route eventually became the most important fur trade corridor between Lake Superior and the West. The trip begins with the famous and arduous *Grande Portage*; from here west to Rainy Lake the surrounding wilderness has remained virtually unchanged since the days of the voyageurs. Impressive geological features in the first 120 kilometres of the trip include the Cascades, a deep gorge through which the Pigeon River cuts; the 200-metre cliffs surrounding Rose Lake; and Silver Falls on Saganaga Lake. Studded with many small, rock-outcrop islands, several of the lakes along this route typify Canadian Shield landscape, and the route passes through the extreme northern limit for some hardwoods, including oak, red maple, basswood and elm. In the final 100 kilometres, from Fort Frances to the town of Rainy River, settlement varies from sparse to dense, and land use is largely agricultural. In this stretch are the archaeologically rich Long Sault Mounds, the burial grounds of an Indian civilization that existed along the Rainy River for over a thousand years. Some especially fine pictographs can also be seen along the way. The pelicans in the Lake of the Woods area at the far western end of the trip are the most unusual wildlife, but ospreys and bald eagles may also be sighted.

Sections of the Boundary Waters are well travelled, particularly in Quetico Provincial Park. West of Fort Frances most of the Rainy River is unfit for either drinking or swimming due to pollution. This route can be extended 160 kilometres to Kenora via a difficult trip on Lake of the Woods. Fishing: lake trout, pickerel, pike, bass.

Route (2) Kaministikwia River Fur Trade

Type River and lake route

Rating A A A B

Length 520 km / 25 days

Portages 23 + / 3 km, 4 km, 13 km, 4 km

Main bodies of water Kaministikwia River, Dog Lake, Lac des Mille Lacs, Pickerel and Sturgeon Lakes, Maligne River, Lac la Croix, Namakan and Rainy Lakes

Start Thunder Bay by road (Hwy 11/17)

Finish Fort Frances by road (Hwy 11)

Intermediate access Kakabeka Falls and Raith by road (Hwy 17), Quetico Provincial Park (French Lake campgrounds) by road (Hwy 11)

Roads, railways and hydro dams have altered the character of this historic route, particularly between Thunder Bay and Lac des Mille Lacs. Several portages have been destroyed or severed by roads or logging operations. Until 1821 this route was of prime importance as a fur-trading corridor. In the early 1870s a section known as the Dawson Trail was used to transport troops and settlers to the Red River area in Manitoba. Today, highlights of this route include the moderately populated Thunder Bay-to-Dog Lake section, which features a spectacular thirty-seven-metre waterfall in Kakabeka Falls Provincial Park, and the wilderness stretch through Quetico Provincial Park. The last third of this trip coincides with a section of the Boundary Waters Fur Trade route (1). Vegetation is varied; some large elms along the Kaministikwia River give way to mixed deciduous-coniferous forest and swamp along the Dog River, and Quetico hardwoods are interspersed with significant stands of red and white pine.

The Kaministikwia and Maligne Rivers have dangerous falls and rapids. Water levels may be low in the Kaministikwia River after late June. Campsites are in limited supply in some sections. Drinking water should be treated. Fishing: pike, pickerel, bass, trout.

Detailed information *The Boundary Waters Fur Trade Canoe Route*

Source Ministry of Natural Resources, Box 5000, Thunder Bay F, Ontario P7E 6E3

Detailed information *Kaministikwia River Fur Trade Canoe Route*

Source Ministry of Natural Resources, Box 5000, Thunder Bay F, Ontario P7E 6E3

Route (3) Kakagi Lake Loop

Type Lake route

Rating n/a B C B

Length 52 km / 4 days

Portages 6 / 2.4 km (wet and muddy in places)

Main bodies of water Kakagi and Cedartree Lakes, Cedartree River, Flint, Stephen and Cameron Lakes

Start / Finish Kakagi Lake by road (off Hwy 71)

Called Crow Lake by local residents, Kakagi is a large, spring-fed body of water with excellent swimming and fishing. This circular route, with an abandoned gold mine on the east shore of Kakagi Lake and Indian pictographs on Stephen Lake, provides good canoeing for the novice. Except for cottages on Kakagi Lake and a tourist camp on Cameron Lake near the end of the trip, these rock-edged waters lie in country frequented only by moose, bear, deer, beaver and other wildlife.

Numerous campsites are available. The long portage from Cameron Lake to Kakagi Lake may pose some difficulty. Fishing: pickerel, pike, perch, trout, muskellunge.

Route (4) Vermilion Bay-Whitefish Bay Loop

Type Lake route

Rating n/a B B A

Length 160 km / 10 days

Portages 17 / 6.5 km (transport may be available), 1.6 km

Main bodies of water Vermilion Bay, Teggau, Dryberry, Berry, Dogpaw, Caviar, Atikwa, Populos, Hawkcliff and Eagle Lakes

Start / Finish Vermilion Bay by road (Hwy 17)

Intermediate access Sioux Narrows by road (Hwy 71)

This route circles through large and small lakes in virtually uninhabited country. Sheer 100-metre cliffs tower over Teggau Lake, which has a recorded depth of over 200 metres. Deep, clear water makes for impressive canoeing throughout the trip. Indian rock paintings decorate cliffs on three of the lakes, and the Pawitik Co-op Indian Village stands on the shore of Whitefish Bay near the halfway point. An abandoned Falconbridge nickel mine can be reached from Populos Lake.

Vermilion Bay is relatively large and requires caution in windy weather. Log booms may block the way in Dryberry and Berry Lakes. Some portages are strenuous. Numerous campsites line the route. This trip can be terminated by passing through Whitefish Bay to Regina Bay and the village of Sioux Narrows. Fishing: lake trout, pickerel, pike; muskellunge in Eagle Lake.

Detailed information *Kenora Canoe Route 8*

Source Ministry of Natural Resources, Box 5080, 808 Robertson Street, Kenora, Ontario P9N 3X9

Detailed information *Kenora Canoe Route 9*

Source Ministry of Natural Resources, Box 5080, 808 Robertson Street, Kenora, Ontario P9N 3X9

Route (5) Rushing River-Sioux Narrows Loop

Type Lake route

Rating n/a B B B

Length 96 km / 6 to 8 days

Portages 12 / 1 km, 1.2 km, 1.6 km

Main bodies of water Dogtooth, Kilvert, Highwind, Hillock, Dryberry and Berry Lakes, Lake of the Woods, Rushing River

Start / Finish Rushing River Provincial Park by road (Hwy 71)

This circle route winds through both cottage country and uninhabited stretches. Some of the lakes are exceptionally clear, and sand beaches and prominent rock formations mark the shore along much of the route. Dryberry Lake is an excellent canoeing lake, dotted with islands and good campsites. Old logging camps can be found on some of the islands. A side trip from Dryberry Lake to Berry Lake offers a good rush of rapids, waterfalls and fast water, but almost no suitable campsites. The south end of Berry Lake falls away into rapids, a few of which can be handled by experienced canoeists. The passage into Lake of the Woods touches Sioux Narrows Provincial Park. The numerous islands of this lake are ideal for camping; there are also many commercial lodges along this section. Indian rock paintings, over 300 years old, decorate the shoreline of Route Bay.

During August, Lake of the Woods usually has a heavy algae cover, and canoeists should carry a supply of drinking water. Fishing: trout, pike, pickerel, muskellunge.

Route (6) Rushing River to Aulneau Peninsula Loop

Type Lake route

Rating n/a B B B

Length 64 km / 5 days

Portages 8

Main bodies of water Rushing River, Lake of the Woods

Start / Finish Rushing River Provincial Park by road (Hwy 71)

Circling through a scenic maze of islands in the northeast corner of Lake of the Woods, this route is laced with shoreline ridges of exposed bedrock. There are rock paintings on Blindfold Lake and wild rice fields near Blueberry Inlet. Large soapstone deposits, once a source of carving stone for the Ojibway, can be seen on Pipestone Peninsula. Some cottages and tourist camps are scattered along the route.

Open stretches of Lake of the Woods can become dangerously rough in windy weather. Poison ivy flourishes here, especially near portages. This trip can be extended from the Hades Islands to Kenora. Fishing: pike, pickerel, muskellunge.

Detailed information *Kenora Canoe Route 15*

Source Ministry of Natural Resources, Box 5080, 808 Robertson Street, Kenora, Ontario P9N 3X9

Detailed information *Kenora Canoe Route 24*

Source Ministry of Natural Resources, Box 5080, 808 Robertson Street, Kenora, Ontario P9N 3X9

Route (7) Dogtooth-Kilvert-White Lake Loop

Type Lake route

Rating n/a B B B

Length 30 km / 2 to 3 days

Portages 5 / 1 km

Main bodies of water Dogtooth, White and Kilvert Lakes

Start / Finish Rushing River Provincial Park by road (Hwy 71)

Intermediate access Dogtooth Lake by road (Kilvert Lake Road)

Sand beaches, a bald eagle's nest and good fishing make Kilvert Lake a high point of this circular trip. Dogtooth Lake is an easy, scenic paddle; there are some cottages along its shore. Low rock cliffs mark the west shore of Portage Lake, a small body of water, and on the south shore of White Lake are more sand beaches.

The open stretches of Kilvert Lake should be avoided in windy weather. Drinking water from Swamp Lake should be treated. Fishing: pike, pickerel, muskellunge, lake trout.

Route (8) Kenora-Fort St. Charles Loop

Type Lake route

Rating n/a B C B

Length 135 km / 10 days

Portages 1

Main body of water Lake of the Woods

Start / Finish Kenora by road (Hwy 17)

Tracing a long, narrow loop through an island-strewn northern section of Lake of the Woods, this route passes through an area rich in the history of the Ojibway. On Kennedy Island petroglyphs depict hunting scenes, animals and symbols significant to the nomadic Indians who once hunted and fished in this area. Other reminders of the native culture include the pictographs of Picture Rock and an old Indian campsite on Fox Island. The European fur trade of the early eighteenth century left Fort St. Charles on Magnusson's Island, the approximate halfway point of this trip. Numerous cottages and tourist camps are scattered throughout the lake, but there are good campsites on quiet inlets and islands. The southern edge of this route follows the Canada-U.S. international boundary.

Lake of the Woods can become very rough. During August this lake usually has a heavy algae cover, and drinking water should be carried. Fishing: pike, pickerel, whitefish, bass.

Detailed information *Kenora Canoe Route 16*

Source Ministry of Natural Resources, Box 5080, 808 Robertson Street, Kenora, Ontario P9N 3X9

Detailed information *Kenora Canoe Route 23*

Source Ministry of Natural Resources, Box 5080, 808 Robertson Street, Kenora, Ontario P9N 3X9

Route (9) Kenora-Cygnet Lake Loop

Type Lake and river route

Rating B B B B

Length 128 km / 10 days

Portages 17

Main bodies of water Louise, Pickerel, Pelicanpouch, Cygnet, Swan, Tetu, Roughneck, Sand and Gun Lakes, Winnipeg River

Start / Finish Kenora by road (Hwy 17)

Two power dams and a few scattered cottages are the only signs of civilization on these waterways, which once served as a link in the fur trade. Distinctive formations of exposed bedrock add to the natural beauty.

Fishing: pickerel, pike.

Route (10) Blue Lake Loop

Type Lake route

Rating C B B B

Length 97 km / 5 to 7 days

Portages 19

Main bodies of water Blue, Langton, Alexandra, Edward, Whitney, Cobble, Gordon, Little Gordon, Daniels, Canyon and Forest Lakes

Start / Finish Blue Lake Provincial Park by road (Hwy 647)

Intermediate access Gordon, McIntosh, Edward and Alexandra Lakes by road (logging roads)

Sandy beaches on Little Gordon Lake, high cliffs, good fishing and an abandoned mica mine on Cobble Lake are features of this route. A few cottages and tourist camps are scattered along the way.

Fishing: lake trout, pickerel, pike.

Detailed information *Kenora Canoe Route 25*

Source Ministry of Natural Resources, Box 5080, 808 Robertson Street, Kenora, Ontario P9N 3X9

Detailed information *Blue Lake Loop*

Source Ministry of Natural Resources, Box 3000, Dryden, Ontario P8N 3B3

Route (11) Upper Wabigoon-English River

Type Lake and river route

Rating B B C A

Length 150 km / 7 days

Portages 13

Main bodies of water Clay Lake, Wabigoon and English Rivers

Start Clay Lake by road (Hwy 609)

Finish Ear Falls by road (Hwy 105)

Intermediate access Ministry of Natural Resources camping area on Wabigoon River by road (Jones Road off Hwy 17)

Indian rock paintings on Ball Lake, two tourist camps and plentiful campsites are features of this former Hudson's Bay Company fur trade route.

Fishing: pickerel, pike.

Route (12) Red Lake-Longlegged Lake Loop

Type Lake and river route

Rating A B B A

Length 224 km / 7 to 12 days

Portages 24 / 1.4 km (steep for first 300 m), 1.9 km (sharp drops and rises)

Main bodies of water Pakwash, Red and Longlegged Lakes

Start / Finish Pakwash Provincial Park by road (off Hwy 105)

Intermediate access Red Lake by road (Hwy 105)

Parts of this route were used to bring supplies to Red Lake before the highway was built. Cottages and tourist camps will be found along the way.

Extra precautions should be taken on the English River system because of fluctuations in the water level from Manitou Dam and Ear Falls. Fishing: pickerel, pike, lake trout.

Detailed information *Kenora Canoe Route 3*

Source Ministry of Natural Resources, Box 5080, 808 Robertson Street, Kenora, Ontario P9N 3X9

Detailed information *Canoe Route 74*

Source Ministry of Natural Resources, Box 323, Red Lake, Ontario P0V 2M0

Route (13) Red Lake-Carroll Lake

Type Lake route

Rating n/a B A B

Length 137 km / 5 to 9 days

Portages 19

Main bodies of water Red, Douglas, Telescope, Hanson, Donald and Carroll Lakes

Start Red Lake by road (Hwy 105)

Finish Carroll Lake by air (or route can be retraced to start)

This route ends in the wilderness at the Ontario-Manitoba boundary, but the trip can be extended across the border to Lake Winnipeg. Evidence of an old Indian encampment can be found on Glenn Lake. Moose, caribou and black bear inhabit the area. Human encounters are relatively common because of tourist and outpost camps along the way.

The large lakes, particularly Red Lake, can be very rough in windy weather. Fishing: pickerel, pike, lake trout.

Detailed information *Red Lake-Carroll Lake Canoe Route*

Source Ministry of Natural Resources, Box 323, Red Lake, Ontario P0V 2M0

Route (14) Pakwash-Trout-Bruce Lake Loop

Type Lake and river route

Rating B A A B

Length 274 km / 13 to 20 days

Portages 26 / 3.4 km, 1.7 km

Main bodies of water Pakwash, Red, Little Vermilion, Nungesser, Coli, Trout and Bruce Lakes

Start / Finish Pakwash Provincial Park by road (off Hwy 105)

Intermediate access Red Lake by road (Hwy 105)

Woodland caribou and several bald eagle nesting sites are attractions along this heavily forested wilderness route. Impressive geological features include Big Falls on Trout Lake River and Trout Lake Ridge, a large esker on the western shore of Trout Lake. Remains of an old wooden dam, once used in the logging industry to raise the water level on Little Vermilion Lake, still stand on the Chukuni River. Settlement in the area is limited to small towns near the beginning of the route, cottages on the Chukuni River and tourist camps on several of the lakes.

Canoes should keep close to shore when travelling the larger bodies of water, particularly Trout Lake. Good campsites are limited in some sections. Fishing: pickerel, pike, lake trout.

Detailed information *Canoe Route 75*

Source Ministry of Natural Resources, Box 323, Red Lake, Ontario P0V 2M0

Route (15) Sioux Lookout or Lake St. Joseph to Red Lake

Type Lake and river route

Rating B A B A

Length 267 to 400 km / 8 to 18 days

Portages 6 to 11

Main bodies of water Lake St. Joseph, Lac Seul, Red Lake

Start Osnaburgh House by road (Hwy 599) or Sioux Lookout by road (Hwy 72) or rail (VIA)

Finish Red Lake by road (Hwy 105)

Intermediate access Ear Falls by road (Hwy 105)

Originally used by native people and later by Hudson's Bay Company men trading in the Red Lake and English River country, this route saw heavy use from the 1920s till the mid 1940s as a mover of men and supplies into what was then the world's most productive gold-mining area around Red Lake. Remains of many of the large overland portage tracks can still be seen at Ear Falls and on portages along the Chukuni River.

The route has a dual starting point, either at Osnaburgh House or Sioux Lookout, the two alternatives converging on Lac Seul. From here the trip can be continued to Red Lake or points on the English River in the Kenora Forest District and on into Manitoba. During low water many beaches are exposed on Lac Seul, and both this lake and Lake St. Joseph can give trouble with their windy, open stretches and myriad confusing island channels and flooded headlands. Fishing: pickerel, pike.

Route (16) Press Lake to Sioux Lookout

Type Lake and river route

Rating B B C B

Length 84 km / 5 days

Portages 10

Main bodies of water Press Lake, English River, Minnitaki, Abram and Pelican Lakes

Start Press Lake by road (Great Lakes Paper Company Road off Hwy 599)

Finish Sioux Lookout by road (Hwy 72) or rail (VIA)

This trip combines the abundant white water, rapids and falls of the English River with scenic lake travel, particularly on Minnitaki Lake, which offers sand beaches, rocky shorelines and numerous islands. Settlement is limited to the village of Sioux Lookout.

Many good campsites are located on Minnitaki and Loggers Lakes. Fishing: pike, pickerel; lake trout, muskellunge in Minnitaki Lake.

Detailed information *Sioux Lookout or Lake St. Joseph to Red Lake*

Source Ministry of Natural Resources, Box 309, Sioux Lookout, Ontario P0V 2T0

Detailed information *Press Lake to Sioux Lookout Canoe Route*

Source Ministry of Natural Resources, Box 309, Sioux Lookout, Ontario P0V 2T0

Route (17) Savant Lake-Sioux Lookout Loop

Type Lake and river route

Rating B A B A

Length 435 km / 22 days

Portages 48 / 3 between 1 and 1.5 km

Main bodies of water Savant, Pashkokogan, Miniss and Hooker Lakes, Marchington and Sturgeon Rivers

Start / Finish Savant Lake by road (Hwy 599) or rail (VIA)

Intermediate access Medcalf Lake by road (Hwy 599), Sioux Lookout by road (Hwy 72) or rail (VIA)

Canoed by French explorers in the late eighteenth century, these waterways still flow through a virtually uninhabited wilderness of winding rivers, rock-lined lakes and dense forest. Settlement is limited to Savant Lake, Osnaburgh House and Sioux Lookout. Wild rice grows at points along the Savant River, and moose, bears, beavers, martens, otters and bald eagles live throughout the area.

Fishing: pickerel, pike.

Route (18) Upper Albany River

Type Lake and river route

Rating A A B A

Length 470 km / 20 to 30 days

Portages 39

Main bodies of water Marchington River, Miniss Lake, Albany River

Start Sioux Lookout by road (Hwy 72) or rail (VIA)

Finish Fort Hope by air

Intermediate access Osnaburgh Lake by road (Hwy 599) or Pickle Lake by road (Hwy 599)

This isolated route offers an impressive variety of canoeing conditions, including slow, swampy rivers, thundering white water and quiet lakes. The topography ranges from sandy beaches to rocky cliffs. Once a major link in the fur trade route connecting Manitoba and northwestern Ontario to Hudson Bay, these waters flow through virtually untouched wilderness.

Supplies are limited to the population clusters at Sioux Lookout, Osnaburgh House and Fort Hope. The trip can be extended to James Bay. (See Route 25.) Fishing: pike, pickerel.

Detailed information *Savant Lake-Sioux Lookout Loop Canoe Route*
Source Ministry of Natural Resources,
Box 309, Sioux Lookout, Ontario P0V 2T0

Detailed information *Albany River: Sioux Lookout to Fort Hope*
Source Ministry of Natural Resources,
Box 309, Sioux Lookout, Ontario P0V 2T0

Route (19) Lake St. Joseph to Menako Lakes

Type Lake and river route

Rating B B B A

Length 190 km / 9 days

Portages 21 / 1.5 km

Main bodies of water Lake St. Joseph, Ochig and Pickle Lakes, Kawinogans River, Badesdawa Lake, Spruce River, Menako Lakes

Start Lake St. Joseph by road (Hwy 599)

Finish Menako Lakes by road (Hwy 808)

Intermediate access Pickle Lake by road (Hwy 599), Badesdawa Lake by road (Hwy 808)

This rarely travelled route winds through black spruce forest, with settlement only at Pickle Lake and New Osnaburgh House. Remnants of gold-mining operations still stand north of Pickle Lake.

Campsites are limited, and a day's journey is usually based on the distance between available campsites. Discoloration of the water is due to natural conditions, not man-made pollutants. Fishing: pickerel, pike.

Route (20) Kawinogans-Bow-Otoskwin Loop

Type River and lake route

Rating B B B A

Length 225 km / 10 to 14 days

Portages 27

Main bodies of water Kawinogans Lake, Kawinogans, Bow and Otoskwin Rivers, Badesdawa Lake

Start / Finish Pickle Lake by road (Hwy 599)

Intermediate access Badesdawa Lake by road (Hwy 808)

A variety of wildlife thrives in the isolated black spruce forest of this little-used route. Human settlement will be found only at the town of Pickle Lake.

The water is discolored by natural elements of the northern environment; there are no man-made pollutants. Campsites are numerous. Fishing: pickerel, pike; sturgeon in Bow Lake and the Otoskwin River.

Detailed information *Lake St. Joseph to Menako Lakes Canoe Route*
Source Ministry of Natural Resources,
Box 309, Sioux Lookout, Ontario P0V 2T0

Detailed information *Kawinogans-Bow-Otoskwin Loop*
Source Ministry of Natural Resources,
Box 309, Sioux Lookout, Ontario P0V 2T0

Route (21) Gull River

Type River and lake route

Rating A C B B

Length 140 km / 7 to 10 days

Portages 20

Main bodies of water Mooseland Lake, Mooseland River, Garden Lake, Gull River

Start Mooseland Lake by road (Dog River Road off Hwy 17)

Finish Gull River Bridge by road (Hwy 527)

Intermediate access Mooseland River by road (Hwy 527)

This isolated wilderness route offers experienced canoeists long stretches of open lake paddling and many difficult rapids. Much of the Gull River is prime moose territory, and west of the river is Devil's Crater, an intriguing geological phenomenon of uncertain origin.

Many of the rapids can be run and some can be lined. Good campsites are limited along the entire length of this infrequently travelled route. Drinking water should be treated. Fishing: pike, pickerel, brook trout.

Detailed information *Gull River Canoe Route*

Source Ministry of Natural Resources, Box 5000, Thunder Bay F, Ontario P7E 6E3

Area (A) Quetico Provincial Park

Type Lake routes

Length Numerous routes possible / 64 to 200 km / 3 to 20 days

Main bodies of water French, Pickerel, Sturgeon, Kawnipi, Agnes, Cirrus, Saganaga and Basswood Lakes

Access By road through any one of three ranger stations off Hwy 11 or through four ranger stations along the Ontario-U.S. border

Over 4500 square kilometres of rolling Shield wilderness and hundreds of kilometres of interconnected lakes and rivers have given Quetico Provincial Park a worldwide canoeing reputation. Many of the portages and campsites in use today were established centuries ago by Indians, whose reddish-brown pictographs of animals and men dot many rock faces in the park. In the fur trade era these waterways linked Quebec and the Great Lakes to the fur riches of the forests and plains farther west. Canadian adventurers, such as Simon Fraser and Alexander Mackenzie, passed through Quetico en route to the Pacific. With the coming of the railway in the early 1900s, lumbermen found easy access to the great red and white pine of the area; lumbering continued in the park until 1971, when it was stopped because of public outcry. Most of the canoeing in the park is on lakes, whose rocky shores are interrupted here and there by sand beaches. Portages are of moderate length and difficulty. Since most of the park is covered with roadless forest and help may be difficult to summon, all canoeists should be fit and experienced campers and paddlers.

Parking for vehicles is provided at each ranger station off Hwy 11. Only reusable food containers are permitted in Quetico Park; ordinary tin cans and glass bottles are prohibited. The use of outboard motors, except by qualified members of the Lac la Croix Indian band, is also prohibited. Canoeists can reserve entry into the park by writing to the address below. Fishing: bass, pickerel, pike; lake trout in deep waters.

Detailed information *Quetico Park Map* ($2.00). This waterproof map does not list individual routes; canoeists must create their own.

Source Ministry of Natural Resources, Quetico Provincial Park, Atikokan, Ontario P0T 1C0

Area (B) Atikokan

Type Lake and river routes

Length 12 documented routes / 36 to 166 km / 3 to 10 days

Main bodies of water Seine River, White Otter and Clearwater West Lakes

Access Atikokan by road (Hwy 11B), Clearwater West Lake by road (Bending Lake Road)

Located just north of Quetico Provincial Park, this area offers a rich variety of canoeing opportunities; lake-to-lake routes, river routes and river and lake routes are all possible, with a good selection of both linear and circular trips. The area includes stretches of remote wilderness and, in the southern portion, some cottages and industry. One route stays within a few kilometres of telephones and other comforts. Man-made attractions of the area include old logging camps, a stock of rainbow trout in Clearwater West Lake, Indian pictographs and the Wilderness Castle on White Otter Lake. This three-storey log building was constructed single-handedly by Jim McQuat in the early 1900s in anticipation of a bride who never came.

The larger lakes are subject to rapid weather changes. High winds can come up quickly and make the larger bodies of water extremely rough and hazardous. Some rapids and small falls may not be marked on the maps and can appear unexpectedly around bends in the rivers. Fishing: lake trout, pickerel, pike, bass.

Detailed information *Atikokan Canoe Routes*. This brochure gives a general description of the area. Descriptions of specific routes can be found in the following brochures.

No. 1 Clearwater West Lake to English River
112 km / 5 days / 22 portages
This route follows large lakes and small, winding creeks; it takes the canoeist to the Wilderness Castle described above.

No. 2 Clearwater Circle Routes through Pekagoning Lake
63 km / 8 days / 35 portages
These waterways offer three circle routes of thirty-six, fifty-four and sixty-five kilometres through seldom-visited areas.

No. 3 Eye River to Clearwater West Lake
72 km / 8+ days / 11 portages
This route passes through some of the most scenic country in the Atikokan district. The estimate of 8+ days includes return to starting point.

No. 4 Marmion Lake Circle Route
56 km / 2 to 4 days / 5 portages
This route starts and ends in Lower Seine Bay.

No. 5 Atikokan to Lac des Mille Lacs and Return
166 km / 8 to 10 days / 37 portages
This route offers a mixture of river and lake travel.

No. 6 Seine River Route (Lac des Mille Lacs to Atikokan)
160 km / 8 days / 24 portages
This route passes through near virgin forest, fire-seared blowdowns, cut-over areas and plantations. The river flows by reminders of the logging history of the area, including rotting bridges and relics of old bush camps.

No. 7 Seine River Route (Atikokan to Fort Frances)
152 km / 5 to 10 days / 5 portages
On this route one is always within a few kilometres of a telephone. Boaters and cottages are frequent.

No. 8 Clearwater West Lake to Ignace
64 km / 5 days / 16 portages
The Wilderness Castle is a highlight of this route, and Indian rock paintings can also be found on White Otter Lake.

No. 9 Wasp Lake Circle Route
90 km / 4 to 6 days / 15 portages
Beautiful scenery and good fishing are attractions on this route.

No. 10 Nym Lake Circle Route
91 km / 4 to 6 days / 32 portages
This route features lake and river canoeing through built-up areas and wilderness.

Source Ministry of Natural Resources,
108 Saturn Avenue, Atikokan, Ontario P0T 1C0

Area (C) White Otter

Type Lake routes

Length 4 documented routes / 27 to 120 km / 2 to 10 days

Main bodies of water Agimak, White Otter, Nora, Elsie, Sandford, Irene, Gulliver and Wabigoon Lakes, English and Turtle Rivers

Access Ignace, Dinorwic, Dryden and English River by road (Hwy 17)

Loggers and trappers are still active in this area of bedrock hills, ridges, black spruce swamps and occasional stands of red and white pine. Human settlement is limited to a few tourist and outpost camps. White Otter Lake is famous for its deep, clear trout waters and for the three-storey log "castle" on its shores. Built in the early 1900s by one man, Jim McQuat, this rare wilderness structure includes a twelve-metre log tower.

Extra caution is required on the larger lakes. Drinking water should be treated. Campsites are common and usually located at portages. Fishing: pickerel, pike, lake trout.

Detailed information *White Otter Canoe Routes*. This brochure gives a general description of the area. Descriptions of specific routes can be found in the following brochures.

No. 103 Ignace to White Otter Lake
35 km / 2 to 3 days / 14 portages
The White Otter Wilderness Castle and good fishing and wildlife viewing are attractions on this trip through a chain of lakes.

No. 103A White Otter Lake to Dryden
120 km / 6 to 8 days / 9 portages

No. 103B Nora Lake to English River
96 km / 5 to 7 days / 16 portages

No. 103C White Otter Lake to Clearwater West Lake
27 km / 1 to 2 days / 1 portage

These three routes are the major variations for continuing Route 103.

Source Ministry of Natural Resources,
Box 448, Ignace, Ontario P0T 1T0

Area (D) Fort Frances

Type Lake routes

Length 16 documented routes / 35 to 150 km / 2 to 14 days

Main bodies of water Rainy Lake, Rainy River, Lake of the Woods

Access Numerous points by road off Hwys 11, 71, 613, 615

Comprised mainly of lake routes, this area offers a few circle trips and convenient road access. Originally travelled by the Cree and Ojibway, these waterways became a link in the fur trade from Lake Superior to the West. Around 1900, sawmills were built, and a pulp and paper mill was later established in Fort Frances. Coniferous forests dominate the Shield landscape, but west of Fort Frances along the Rainy River the typical granite outcrops and shallow soils give way to a strip of agricultural land that stretches to Lake of the Woods.

Paddling on Rainy Lake and Lake of the Woods requires special caution. Drinking water should be treated. Fishing: pike, pickerel, smallmouth bass, largemouth bass, muskellunge.

Detailed information

No. 1 Nestor Falls Circle Route via Kakagi Lake
105 km / 3 to 6 days / 13 portages
Beginning and ending in a heavily populated area, this route passes through rugged wilderness with clear waters and sand beaches.

No. 2 Caliper Lake to Burditt Lake
51 km / 3 to 4 days / 3 portages
Easy portaging and paddling make this a good family route.

No. 3 Caliper Lake to Burditt Lake via Pipestone Lake
102 km / 5 to 7 days / 7 portages
This is a wilderness route without strenuous paddling.

No. 4 Burditt Lake Loop
89 km / 4 to 5 days / 6 portages
Excellent wildlife viewing and good fishing highlight this route.

No. 5 Clearwater to Lake Despair
83 km / 4 to 8 days / 3 portages
Beaver lodges, herons and the occasional bald eagle are seen here.

No. 6 Lake Despair Circle Route
48 km / 2 to 5 days / 4 portages
This rugged route follows two small, shallow rivers and contends with the inevitable winds on open lakes.

No. 7 Rainy Lake Loop
144 km / 7 to 10 days / 15 portages
This route offers many excellent campsites in scenic settings.

No. 8 Hickerson Lake to Cuttle Lake
75 km / 2 to 5 days / 5 portages
There is good fishing and wildlife viewing here as well as an abundance of rocky points that offer sheltered camping. A good family route.

No. 9 Vickers Lake to Fort Frances via the Big Canoe River
123 km / 6 to 10 days / 12 portages
Ideal fishing and the scenery on Vista Lake are highpoints of this trip.

No. 10 Vickers Lake to Fort Frances via the Manitou River
112 km / 5 to 7 days / 8 portages
Deep lakes and river rapids are features of this wilderness trip.

No. 11 Vickers Lake to Lower Manitou and Return
48 km / 2 to 4 days / 5 portages
There is exceptional scenery on Vickers Lake.

No. 12 Vickers Lake to Laver
52 km / 2 to 5 days / 14 portages
This route passes through rugged bush landscape, with scenic campsites on lake islands. Portages can make for a hard day's work.

No. 13 Vickers via Lower Manitou, Scattergood, Eaglerock, Sakwite Lake and Otukamanoan
120 km / 5 to 14 days / 21 portages
This rugged and extremely beautiful trip features both river and open lake paddling. It is recommended for fit, experienced canoeists.

No. 14 Mine Centre to Redgut Bay
35 km / 2 to 3 days / 2 portages
Both open water and narrow river travel mark this route. Rapids require some whitewater experience. Good camping on sand beaches.

No. 15 Lower Seine River Canoe Route
136 km / 5 to 7 days / 3 portages
Signs of early logging, mining and electricity development are found along this lake and river route.

No. 16 Clearwater West to Little Turtle Lake
150 km / 6 to 10 days / 16 portages
The camping varies from excellent to nonexistent along this route. The shoreline is swampy and inaccessible in some sections.

Source Ministry of Natural Resources, 922 Scott Street, Fort Frances, Ontario P9A 1J4

Area (E) Dryden

Type Lake and river routes

Length 10 documented routes / 32 to 100 km / 2 to 14 days

Main bodies of water Eagle, Wabigoon and Dinorwic Lakes

Access Numerous points by road in the Dryden area

An intricate system of lakes and rivers twists through the bedrock cliffs and drift-filled valleys of this area. Including some circle trips, these routes offer opportunities for the novice as well as the experienced canoeist. Large red and white pines mark the lake and island shores, and sandy beaches provide good stopovers and swimming. Rapids and portages are relatively infrequent. These waterways have been travelled for over 7000 years by native populations, and Indian pictographs can be found at several locations. These routes also served as arteries during the fur trade era, and abandoned mines are reminders of a minor gold rush in the early 1900s. Though there are some cottages, tourist camps and logging operations, these routes pass through largely uninhabited wilderness.

The large lakes, particularly Eagle, can be extremely hazardous in high winds. Drinking water should be treated. Fishing: pike, pickerel, smallmouth bass, yellow perch, muskellunge, lake trout, sauger.

Detailed information *Dryden Area Canoe Routes*

Source Ministry of Natural Resources,
Box 3000, Dryden, Ontario P8N 3B3

Area (F) Sandbar

Type Lake and river routes

Length 5 documented routes / 112 to 262 km / 5 to 10 days

Main bodies of water Sandbar, Mameigwess, Barrel, Sowden and Brightsand Lakes, English and Brightsand Rivers

Access Sandbar Lake by road (Hwy 599), English River by road (Hwy 17), Gulliver River by road (Hwy 17)

This area offers trips on the English and Brightsand River systems. All routes travel through parts of Sandbar Lake Provincial Park and feature boreal forest and rugged Canadian Shield landscape. Numerous sandy beaches break the generally steep, rocky shores. At points these waterways come into contact with activities of the logging industry. Many variations on the documented routes are possible.

Detailed information

No. 62A English River to Allan Water
198 km / 8 days / 34 portages
This route offers abundant white water, with rapids suited to novice and experienced canoeists. It includes lake and river travel and excellent fishing.

No. 78 Sandbar-Press Lake Loop
160 km / 10 days / 14 portages
This route features varied terrain, large and small lakes, Indian pictographs and good fishing and wildlife viewing.

No. 79 Sandbar Provincial Park Loop
112 km / 5 days / 12 portages
This is a scenic lake and river route with Indian pictographs on two lakes. Beaver dams and larger lakes provide challenges.

No. 80 Hwy 17 to Sandbar Provincial Park
180 km / 8 days / 20 portages
This downstream English River route features varied scenery and abundant rapids. Lake travel predominates after the initial forty kilometres.

No. 81 Sandbar Provincial Park to Sioux Lookout
262 km / 9 days / 22 portages
Island-dotted lakes and the Sturgeon River make up this trip through sparsely populated country. The frequent wide beaches were once used as campsites by Indians, explorers and traders.

Source Ministry of Natural Resources,
Box 448, Ignace, Ontario P0T 1T0

Area (G) Sioux Lookout

Type Lake and river routes

Length 9 documented routes / 115 to 315 km / 4 to 18 days

Main bodies of water Marchington and Hooker Lakes, Vermilion River, Lac Seul

Access Sioux Lookout by road (Hwy 72) or rail (VIA), a few other points by road

This area offers a combination of lake and river travel through a gently rolling and heavily forested landscape. West of Sioux Lookout stands the rise of land that gives the town its name. According to legend, Ojibway Indians placed a lookout here to watch for an attack of Sioux warriors from the south. Sand beaches dot the routes, and sightings of ospreys and bald eagles have been reported.

Caution should be exercised when carrying canoes over railroad tracks. Fishing: northern pike, yellow pickerel.

Area (H) De Lesseps

Type Lake routes

Length 5 documented routes / 77 to 200 km / 3 to 10 days

Main bodies of water Fitchie, Pashkokogan, Medcalf and Minchin Lakes

Access Fitchie, Minchin, Hamilton, Medcalf and Pashkokogan Lakes by road (Hwy 599)

Good fishing is a highlight of all the wilderness routes in this area. Scattered signs of human settlement are limited to the Hwy 599 corridor. Enterprising canoeists can travel a number of undocumented routes from the access points.

Fishing: pike, pickerel.

Detailed information *Sioux Lookout Canoe Area*

Source Ministry of Natural Resources, Box 309, Sioux Lookout, Ontario P0V 2T0

Detailed information *De Lesseps Canoe Area*

Source Ministry of Natural Resources, Box 309, Sioux Lookout, Ontario P0V 2T0

Area (I) Whitewater Lake-Ogoki Reservoir

Type Lake and river routes

Length Numerous routes possible / 50 to 280 km / 3 to 14 days

Main bodies of water Ogoki Reservoir, Ogoki and Allandale Rivers, Whitewater, Whiteclay, Smoothrock, Caribou, Brennan and Granite Lakes

Access Armstrong by road (Hwy 527) or rail (VIA). VIA also stops on request at points east and west of Armstrong.

With an almost equal split between river and lake-to-lake routes, this area offers nearly 1600 kilometres of diversified canoeing. Most of the area lies within the Arctic Watershed, with some routes crossing into the Nipigon drainage basin (Great Lakes-St. Lawrence Watershed). The terrain includes rolling country with large expanses of exposed granite bedrock, sharply broken areas of diabase cliffs and flat lowland areas. Pictographs on some of the lakes are reminders of the Indians who travelled these routes in the past; their ancestors still use the waterways today. The area is rich in wildlife, including caribou, bear, lynx, timber wolf, otter, mink, osprey and bald eagle. Most of the river routes have impressive falls and rapids, and canoeing in this remote area should not be attempted by inexperienced trippers. Although a few outfitters' camps are sprinkled throughout the area, permanent settlement is limited almost completely to a strip along the railroad line. There is some timber extraction in the southeast corner.

Some routes may be affected by low water levels late in the season. Campsites are in limited supply in some sections. All but the simplest stretches of rapids have portages, but in some cases approaches are tricky. Fishing: pike, pickerel, lake trout, brook trout.

Detailed information *Nipigon Canoe Routes* (map). The connecting waterways in this area are divided into approximately fifty sections, which are delineated on this map. After selecting enough sections to create a "route", the canoeist should write a second time to request larger-scale maps and written descriptions for each section.

Source Ministry of Natural Resources,
Box 970, Nipigon, Ontario P0T 2J0

Area (J) Nipigon

Type Lake and river routes

Length Numerous routes possible / 48 to 128 km / 3 to 12 days

Main bodies of water Lake Nipigon, Gull, Kabitotikwia, Black Sturgeon, Nipigon, Blackwater and Sturgeon Rivers

Access Hwy 11 east of Nipigon, Hwy 811 off Hwy 527

These lake and river routes lie within the Great Lakes-St. Lawrence Watershed and flow into Lake Nipigon, the largest lake in northern Ontario after Lake Superior. During the fur trade era many outposts were established on Lake Nipigon, but little evidence of these remains today. Some of the routes involve travel on small lakes, and all offer a variety of conditions, from the rapids, falls and fast water of a rocky, broken terrain to the easy meanderings of flat lowlands. The area has been logged over, and many of the rivers are still used for seasonal log drives. Only the Blackwater River route, which passes through the town of Beardmore, includes a populated stretch.

Caution is always required on Lake Nipigon. Portages are generally short and in good repair. Two power dams on the swift-flowing Nipigon River require portaging. Drinking water from the Blackwater River should be treated. Fishing: pike, pickerel, brook trout.

Detailed information *Nipigon Canoe Routes* (map). This map also includes routes in the Whitewater Lake-Ogoki Reservoir Canoe Area. After selecting a route, the canoeist should write a second time to request larger-scale maps and written descriptions.

Source Ministry of Natural Resources,
Box 970, Nipigon, Ontario P0T 2J0

Area (K) Graham

Type Lake and river routes

Length 9 documented routes / 55 to 176 km / 2 to 10 days

Main bodies of water Brightsand, Kopka and Weaver Rivers, Pakashkan, Harmon, Seseganaga and Metionga Lakes

Access Graham Road off Hwy 17 (160 km west of Thunder Bay), Pakashkan or Mooseland Lake by road (Dog River off Hwy 17), Obonga or Bukemiga Lake by road (Hwy 527)

This area northwest of Thunder Bay offers over 1000 kilometres of canoeing, with routes of varying lengths for the novice as well as the whitewater enthusiast. The interconnecting network of rivers and lakes allows for numerous convenient loop routes. Except for the rugged landscape in the eastern portion, the area is typical boreal forest — rolling countryside heavily treed with spruce and jack pine. The northern edge of this area touches the fringe of an extensive wilderness stretching to Hudson Bay. Evidence of native culture is limited to occasional pictographs. The area was never an important link in the fur trade, but a small trading post can be found on Sturgeon Lake just west of Graham. Although logging camps are the only permanent settlements, recent road construction has marred the wilderness in some sections.

Kopka, Weaver, Gull and Roaring Rivers and Ottertooth Creek all have severe rapids and large waterfalls that require extreme caution. Low water may cause difficulties in late summer. Few portages exceed 300 metres, and there are no crossings of large, open water. Drinking water should be treated. Fishing: pike, pickerel, whitefish.

Detailed information *Graham Area Canoe Routes*. This brochure gives a general description of the area. Descriptions of specific routes can be found in the following brochures.

No. 1 Brightsand River Circle
54 km / 2 to 4 days / 11 portages
Easy portages and numerous campsites make this an excellent trip for inexperienced canoeists.

No. 2 Brightsand River Circle
76 km / 3 to 5 days / 10 portages
Similar to No. 1, this longer route is also a good trip for inexperienced canoeists.

No. 3 Brightsand River Circle
150 km / 5 to 10 days / 19 portages
This wilderness trip, with some fast water, is one of the best circuits in the district.

No. 4 Brightsand River Circle
96 km / 4 to 6 days / 16 portages
The steep shores of the Shikag River and an excellent moose habitat near Dunne Lake are highlights of this wilderness route. Some portages (up to 1.2 kilometres) require good physical condition.

No. 5 Kashishibog River to Brightsand River
160 km / 6 to 10 days / 23 portages
Island-studded Kashishibog Lake, swampy river channels, the wide Brightsand River and sandy beaches on Brightsand Lake are all aspects of this route, which is recommended for experienced, physically fit canoeists.

No. 6 Kashishibog River Circle
112 km / 4 to 7 days / 23 portages
This route travels through some of the most beautiful wilderness in the area. The canoeist will encounter frequent, usually short portages and few developed campsites.

No. 7 Pakashkan Lake Circle
175 km / 6 to 10 days / 19 portages
This long whitewater trip requires strength, extensive canoeing experience and a very durable canoe. Best in late June or early July.

No. 8 Kashishibog River to Bukemiga Lake
144 km / 5 to 8 days / 15 portages
This scenic trip demands considerable canoeing experience. There are some very difficult portages and forty-eight rapids requiring whitewater expertise.

No. 9 Weaver River to Obonga Lake
88 km / 4 to 5 days / 13 portages
The prime attraction on this route is the stretch between Survey and Obonga Lakes, where the river drops 100 metres in a series of waterfalls into a deep canyon. Difficult portages require experience and stamina.

Source Ministry of Natural Resources, Box 5000, Thunder Bay F, Ontario P7E 6E3

Area (L) Northern Light Lake

Type Lake routes

Length 10 documented routes / 32 to 118 km / 2 to 8 days

Main bodies of water Northern Light, Saganaga, Saganagons and Gunflint Lakes, Weikwabinonaw River

Access Northern Light Lake by road (off Hwy 588), Burchell Lake by road (Hwy 11), Shebandowan Lakes by road (Hwy 11), Weikwabinonaw Lake by road (Boreal Timber Road off Hwy 590)

This area offers a series of interconnected lakes set between high hills crowned with red and white pine. Northern Light Lake, the largest of these, is divided by peninsulas and dozens of small islands, which afford excellent campsites and secluded rest stops. Saganaga Lake shares these features, but is more heavily used. Two of the routes follow a short section of the historic Boundary Waters Fur Trade route (1). Attractions in this area include pictographs on Northern Light Lake, a large sand beach on Titmarsh Lake, Silver Falls near the western end of Saganaga Lake and a rustic marine railway between Northern Light and Saganaga Lakes.

Portages are generally short, and the absence of difficult river travel makes this area suitable for novices. Drinking water should be treated. Fishing: pike, pickerel, bass; lake trout in deeper lakes.

Detailed information *Northern Light Lake Canoe Routes*. This brochure gives a general description of the area. Descriptions of specific routes can be found in the following brochures.

No. 1 Northern Light Lake Circle
52 km / 2 to 4 days / 4 portages
This excellent route for canoeists with limited experience features easy portages, pictographs, heavy forest and good fishing.

No. 2 Northern Light Lake Circle
50 km / 2 to 4 days / 11 to 14 portages
This is a well-used route, with some sections of white water. Koss Lake is known for its pickerel and pike fishing, and osprey nests and occasional bald eagles are highlights of wildlife viewing.

No. 3 Northern Light Lake Circle
56 km / 3 to 4 days / 16 portages
This route features scenic rock outcrops and sections of fast water.

No. 4 Northern Light Lake Circle
78 km / 4 to 6 days / 14 to 20 portages
There are two long portages on this route, which follows some of the lakes and rivers used by voyageurs two centuries ago.

No. 5 Northern Light Lake Circle
96 km / 5 to 8 days / 25 portages
This is a little-used route through a chain of lakes. The relatively poor condition of many portages (three are one kilometre in length) requires good physical conditioning and canoe trip experience.

No. 6 Yellowhammer Lake to Hand Lake
43 km / 2 to 3 days / 13 portages
This route offers excellent fishing. There is considerable river travel, but no whitewater experience is required.

No. 7 Burchell Lake to Northern Light Lake
121 km / 5 to 7 days / 18 portages
Several difficult portages (two are one kilometre in length) rule out this route for beginners. There is a varied landscape of rivers, lakes and swamp.

No. 8 Lower Shebandowan Lake to Northern Light Lake
88 km / 5 to 6 days / 10 to 13 portages
Some white water and several long and difficult portages (one requires use of compass) make this a route for experienced canoeists.

No. 9 Matawin River to Lower Shebandowan Lake
46 km / 2 to 3 days / 9 portages
This river and lake route, with rapids, falls and three portages between one and three kilometres, requires considerable lining and wading.

No. 10 Swallow Lake Circle
32 km / 2 days / 3 to 7 portages
This trip through a densely forested area with excellent swimming is ideal for beginners.

Source Ministry of Natural Resources,
Box 5000, Thunder Bay F, Ontario P7E 6E3

Routes 22 to 24

Route

22 Fawn River
23 Winisk River
24 Ekwan River

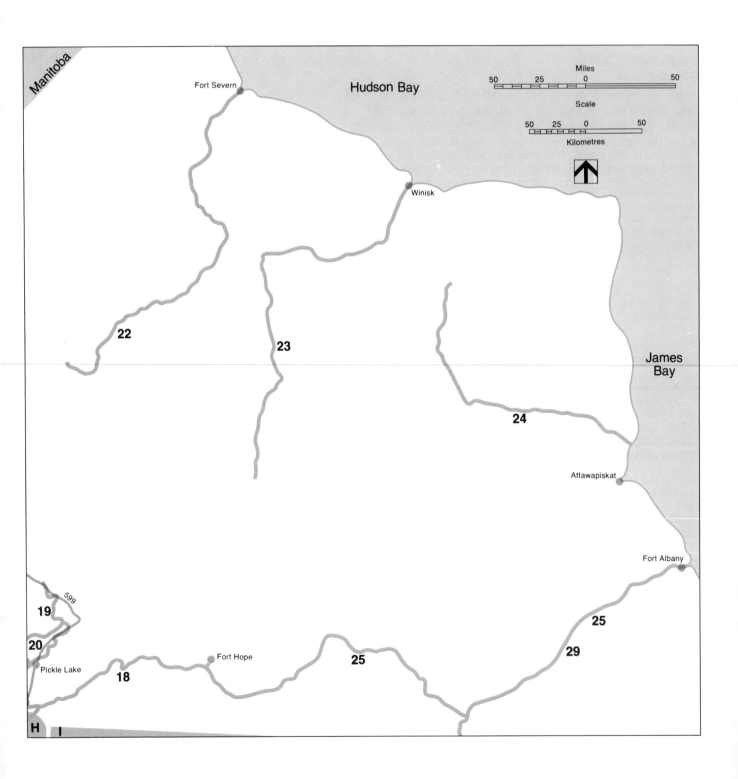

Route (22) Fawn River

Type River route

Rating A B A A

Length 402 km / 10 to 14 days

Portages 18 / 3.2 km, 1 km, 1 km, 1.3 km

Main bodies of water Big Trout Lake, Fawn and Severn Rivers

Start Big Trout Lake by air

Finish Fort Severn by air

This isolated route cuts through Precambrian bedrock to the muskeg and deep peat of the Hudson Bay Lowlands. Labrador tea, sweetgale and fireweed grace the shores; and on open, well-drained areas atop the banks, bear berries and blueberries grow in abundance. Moose, caribou, bears and wolves live in the area, and the final portage on this route offers a good opportunity to find a wide variety of fossils in the limestone of the lower Severn River. Used for centuries by the Big Trout Cree, the Fawn River is dotted with some of their fishing and trapping camps. The remains of a trading post abandoned thirty to fifty years ago stand in a clearing above the last rapids dropping off the Canadian Shield. Below rapids and near old campsites, graves sometimes dot the shore.

This can be a hazardous route, and guides are highly recommended. Portages are difficult to locate and often start within a canoe length of rapids and falls. Raingear and winter clothing are essential. This route should not be travelled before mid June. Fishing: brook trout in rapids; pickerel and pike in tributary streams.

Route (23) Winisk River

Type River route

Rating A B C A

Length 434 km / 10 to 14 days

Portages 9 to 12 / 1.2 km, 350 m (steep and in poor condition)

Main bodies of water Winisk Lake, Winisk River

Start Webequie by air

Finish Winisk by air

This route challenges experienced canoeists with extensive white water and long-distance travel through the solitude of muskeg wilderness. Winisk Lake and virtually all of the Winisk River are protected within a Waterway Provincial Park. For the first 160 kilometres the river runs wild and fast, with many rapids and falls. For the next 160 kilometres it continues to run swiftly, but with fewer sudden rapids. Along the entire route are burnt-over areas with very little mature forest. Near Hudson Bay the river crosses into Polar Bear Provincial Park, which contains one of the southernmost extensions of arctic tundra in the world. Limestone Rapids offers a last dash through white water, and high limestone cliffs, islands and gravel mounds make the final stretch uniquely scenic. The trip ends 6.5 kilometres inland from the Bay.

A guide is strongly recommended. Supplies can be purchased in Webequie and Winisk. Raingear and winter clothing are essential. The last part of the trip will be affected by coastal winds. This river should not be run before June 20. Fishing: pike, pickerel; brook trout in fast water.

Detailed information *Fawn River Canoe Route*

Source Ministry of Natural Resources,
Box 190, Moosonee, Ontario P0L 1Y0

Detailed information *Winisk River Canoe Route*

Source Ministry of Natural Resources,
Box 190, Moosonee, Ontario P0L 1Y0
or
Ministry of Natural Resources,
Box 640, Geraldton, Ontario P0T 1M0

Route (24) Ekwan River

Type River and sea route

Rating A A A A

Length 354 km / 14 days

Portages 2 / 400 m (over muskeg), 6.5 km (over muskeg)

Main bodies of water Hawley and Sutton Lakes, Washagami and Ekwan Rivers, James Bay

Start Hawley Lake by air

Finish Attawapiskat by air

This isolated route winds through the subarctic muskeg country of the Hudson Bay Lowlands. The towering Precambrian outcroppings of the Sutton Ridges are an outstanding geological feature during the early part of the trip. Also impressive are the clear waters and gravel banks of Hawley and Sutton Lakes, which are divided by a massive seventy-five metre gorge. Arctic terns frequent Sutton Lake, and bald and golden eagles have nested on the crags of Sutton Narrows. Wolves and an occasional polar bear inhabit the region. The sod-covered riverbanks nourish ferns and grasses, and fiddleheads make excellent eating. The Washagami River, which is dotted with unusual beaver holes, flows swiftly through narrow clay banks. The Ekwan River is also a fast, narrow waterway. It flows through the abandoned Attawapiskat Indian Reserve, where a large wooden cross, two small graves and a sod-covered winter tepee are of interest. At the end of this trip a sixteen-kilometre paddle along the shallow coast of James Bay reveals the luxuriant growth of the intertidal marshes.

A guide is essential. The swampy terrain requires rubber boots, and raingear and winter clothing are essential. Because of the frigid waters, canoeing should not begin before mid June. Muskeg portaging is extremely strenuous, and travel along the James Bay coast can be difficult and dangerous. Fishing: brook trout, lake trout, whitefish.

Detailed information *Ekwan River Canoe Route*

Source Ministry of Natural Resources, Box 190, Moosonee, Ontario P0L 1Y0

Routes 25 to 38

Route

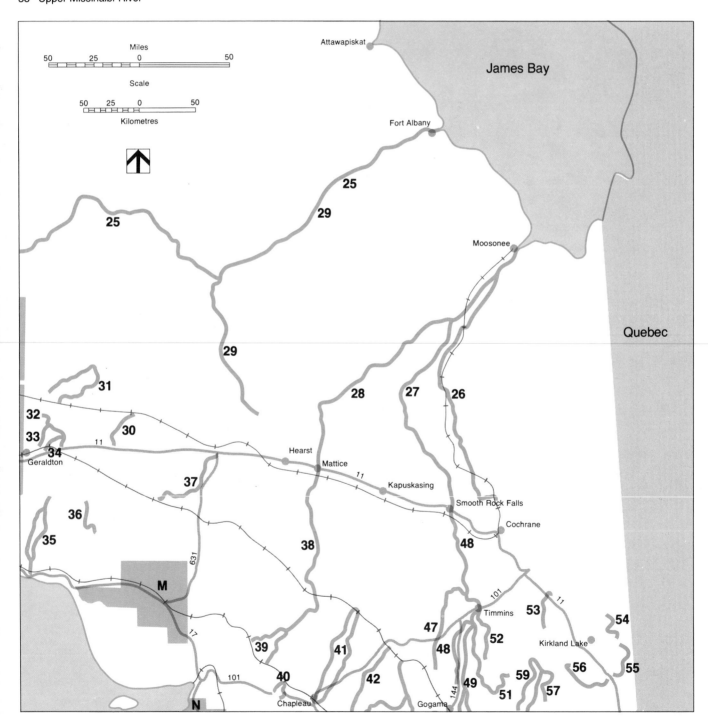

Route (25) Lower Albany River

Type River route

Rating A A B A

Length 610 km / 18 to 20 days

Portages 14 / 200 m (slippery rocks), 75 m (sharp rocks)

Main bodies of water Eabamet Lake, Albany River

Start Fort Hope by air

Finish Fort Albany by air

Recommended for only the most experienced canoeists, this isolated route crosses rolling rock and muskeg country to James Bay. The first half of the trip churns over long stretches of violent rapids and numerous falls. Gradually the river widens, leaving behind its rocky shores, and carves its way through high clay banks on the Hudson Bay Lowlands. Limestone Rapids, on the approach to James Bay, offers a final rush of white water. Islands, tall white cliffs and ice-sculpted piles of gravel mark these final reaches. Winter camps of native trappers are evident along the route. It is imperative that none of their equipment be disturbed.

Although some expert canoeists do travel this route unaided, a guide is recommended. Raingear and winter clothing are essential. The last stretch of the trip will be affected by coastal winds and tides. Fishing: pike, pickerel; brook trout at the bottom of rapids and falls.

Route (26) Abitibi River

Type River route

Rating B B A B

Length 338 km / 10 to 12 days

Portages 5 / 3.2 km (optional), 2.4 km

Main bodies of water Abitibi River, Onakawana River (optional), Moose River

Start Gardiner Ferry by road (Hwy 579), Island Falls by road (Hwy 807)

Finish Moosonee by rail (Ontario Northland)

Intermediate access Abitibi Canyon by road (Hwy 807), Otter Rapids and Moose River Crossing by rail (Ontario Northland)

This historic waterway was once part of an important fur trade route to James Bay. Many of the rapids that once marked the descent of the Abitibi River off the Canadian Shield onto the Hudson Bay Lowlands are now gone; they have been replaced by long stretches of flat water created by hydro dams at Island Falls, Abitibi Canyon and Otter Rapids. However, from Otter Rapids to approximately the mouth of the Onakawana River (a distance of sixty kilometres), the Abitibi River is unnavigable because of shallow water and dangerous rapids. From Otter Rapids the canoeist must either take the train to the Onakawana River bridge or Moose River Crossing or portage three kilometres overland to the Onakawana River and follow it to where it joins the Abitibi River. The Abitibi flows into the broad, powerful Moose River at the Allan Rapids. Another thirty kilometres will bring the canoeist to Moosonee. Moose Factory, on an island in the estuary, was the site of one of the most important Hudson's Bay Company posts.

Below hydro dams, water levels can fluctuate, and canoeists should camp well up the bank. The water of the Abitibi River is muddy ("coffee with cream"), and the best drinking water is obtained from small tributaries. Tidal currents and strong winds can make travel difficult on the lower Moose River. Fishing: pike, pickerel; brook trout in the Onakawana River and its tributaries.

Detailed information *The Albany River Canoe Route*

Source Ministry of Natural Resources,
Box 190, Moosonee, Ontario P0L 1Y0
or
Ministry of Natural Resources,
Box 640, Geraldton, Ontario P0T 1M0

Detailed information *Abitibi River Canoe Route*

Source Ministry of Natural Resources,
Box 730, 2 Third Avenue, Cochrane, Ontario P0L 1C0
or
Ministry of Natural Resources,
Box 190, Moosonee, Ontario P0L 1Y0

Route (27) Lower Mattagami River

Type River route

Rating B B A A

Length 354 km / 10 to 12 days

Portages 5 / 21 km

Main bodies of water Mattagami and Moose Rivers

Start 1 km north of Smooth Rock Falls by road (Hwy 807)

Finish Moosonee by rail (Ontario Northland)

Intermediate access Kipling Dam by road (Hwy 807), Moose River Crossing by rail (Ontario Northland)

This route is the continuation of Route 49. Probably used for centuries by Indians, the Mattagami River later served to bring furs out of the interior to the Hudson's Bay post at Moose Factory. The first third of this route descends off the Shield in clusters of rapids that gradually give way to a lake-like widening of the river behind Little Long Dam. Through the last two-thirds of the route the dark brown Mattagami makes its way across the more level topography of the Hudson Bay Lowlands.

The biggest difficulty on this route is the portage around the stretch between the Little Long Dam and the Kipling Dam. Shallow water and rapids have made this section unnavigable. However, transportation on this portage can be arranged as outlined in the brochure. The best drinking water is available from tributary streams. Tidal currents and strong winds can make travel difficult on the lower Moose River. Fishing: pike, pickerel, sturgeon; brook trout in a few tributary streams.

Route (28) Lower Missinaibi River

Type River route

Rating A B A A

Length 320 km / 7 to 9 days

Portages 7 to 10 / 1 km, 2.8 km, a few arduous shorter portages

Main bodies of water Missinaibi and Moose Rivers

Start Mattice by road (Hwy 11)

Finish Moosonee by rail (Ontario Northland)

Intermediate access Moose River Crossing by rail (Ontario Northland)

This isolated section of the Missinaibi River makes its tortuous way off the Canadian Shield onto the Hudson Bay Lowlands. A moderately difficult trip during high water, the river changes dramatically through summer and early fall. Shoals and boulders complicate progress, and a fine eye for the main channel is necessary. The approach to the turbulent chutes of Thunder House Falls requires extreme caution; the portage must not be missed. The dense bush of the first part of the trip gives way on the Lowlands to high clay banks. Here the river is calmer and wider, though the canoeist still faces a few rapids and seasonal low water difficulties. A maze of islands and winds and tides from James Bay offer a challenge in the final reaches of the Moose River.

This is not a trip for inexperienced canoeists. There are several sections where the only alternative to running rapids are difficult portages. Beware of the turbulence caused by the confluence of large rivers, such as the Mattagami and the Abitibi. Campsites are not always plentiful. Guides can occasionally be employed and some provisions purchased at Mattice. Fishing: pickerel, pike, some brook trout.

Detailed information *Mattagami River Canoe Route (Smooth Rock Falls to Moosonee)*

Source Ministry of Natural Resources,
Box 730, 2 Third Avenue, Cochrane, Ontario P0L 1C0
or
Ministry of Natural Resources,
Box 190, Moosonee, Ontario P0L 1Y0

Detailed information *Missinaibi River (Mattice to Moosonee)*

Source Ministry of Natural Resources,
6 Government Road, Kapuskasing, Ontario P5N 2W4
or
Ministry of Natural Resources,
Box 190, Moosonee, Ontario P0L 1Y0

Route (29) Limestone Rapids to Fort Albany

Type River route

Rating B B n/a A

Length 402 km / 6 days

Portages 0

Main bodies of water Kabinakagami, Kenogami and Albany Rivers

Start Limestone Rapids by road (Rogers Road northwest of Hearst)

Finish Fort Albany by air

Dozens of rapids churn along these isolated rivers, and a steady drop in elevation ensures an active current all the way. An abandoned trading post at Mammamattawa, at the junction of the Kenogami and Kabinakagami Rivers, recalls the history of the Hudson's Bay Company in the area. The Ghost River post on the Albany River still functions during the fall and winter fur trade. Moose, bears and wolves roam the muskeg wilderness, and stands of spruce, birch and poplar are common along the entire route.

Although there are no portages, some of the rapids may need to be lined. At least two sets of bad rapids on the Albany River should be avoided by choosing alternate channels. The Ministry of Natural Resources office in Hearst should be contacted to check water levels in the Kabinakagami River. Campsites are scarce past the mouth of the Current River, and it may be necessary to camp on the rocky riverbank five metres above river level. The last stretch of the trip can be very confusing, and a thorough study of the maps and detailed information is necessary to avoid getting lost for days in a maze of islands and blind channels. The last few kilometres of the trip will be affected by the winds and tides of James Bay. Raingear and winter clothing are essential. Fishing: pickerel, pike, brook trout.

Route (30) Flint River

Type River route

Rating B B C B

Length 48 km / 3 days

Portages 6

Main bodies of water Klotz and Flint Lakes, Flint River

Start Klotz Lake by road (Hwy 11)

Finish Near Flintdale by rail (VIA)

Starting in Klotz Lake Provincial Park, this route offers numerous rapids and small falls running through a forest mix of northern evergreens and hardwoods. Cottages dot the shoreline of Klotz Lake, and two commercial outpost camps are located on Flint Lake. Logging roads are being constructed in the vicinity.

The Flint River becomes quite shallow during the summer months. The canoeist must be alert for a number of rapids and falls not marked as portages on the map; they are simply lift-overs. Fishing: brook trout, pike, pickerel.

Detailed information *Limestone Rapids to Fort Albany*

Source Ministry of Natural Resources,
Box 190, Moosonee, Ontario P0L 1Y0

Detailed information *Flint River Canoe Route*

Source Ministry of Natural Resources,
Box 640, Geraldton, Ontario P0T 1M0

Route (31) Wababimiga-Drowning River

Type Lake and river route

Rating A A A A

Length 140 km / 10 to 15 days

Portages 21 / 2 km, 1.2 km

Main bodies of water Cordingley and Wababimiga Lakes, Wababimiga and Drowning Rivers, Relief and Lower Twin Lakes

Start Cordingley Lake by road (off Hwy 643)

Finish Lower Twin Lake by road (off Hwy 643)

This trip through excellent brook trout waters is one of the most popular routes in the Geraldton district. Rapids and small falls add variety to the river paddling, and there is also canoeing on large, open lakes. Sections of this waterway were originally used by Indians and later by white trappers. Just above Wababimiga Lake scars of the huge 1967 forest fire are still visible. The timber industry operates in this area, and old and new logging roads can be seen at points along the route. Log jams are sometimes large enough to require a portage. Trappers' cabins are located on the rivers and lakes, and cottages dot the shorelines of the larger lakes.

Low water levels in July and August may cause difficulties. Fishing: brook trout in rivers; pickerel, pike in lakes.

Route (32) Kenogami No. 1

Type Lake and river route

Rating B A C A

Length 53 km / 3 days

Portages 4

Main bodies of water Poilu and Burrows Lake, Burrows and Kenogami Rivers

Start Murky Creek by road (Hwy 584)

Finish Longlac by road (Hwy 11)

Good fishing and numerous small falls and rapids make this a pleasant trip through an area of active timber operations. Portages on Ashmore Creek bypass an old dam and the ruins of a logging camp that operated forty years ago.

Low water levels in July and August may cause difficulties. Fishing: pike, pickerel.

Detailed information *Wababimiga-Drowning River Canoe Route*

Source Ministry of Natural Resources, Box 640, Geraldton, Ontario P0T 1M0

Detailed information *Kenogami Canoe Route No. 1*

Source Ministry of Natural Resources, Box 640, Geraldton, Ontario P0T 1M0

Route (33) Kenogami No. 2

Type Lake and river route

Rating B A C A

Length 61 km / 3 to 4 days

Portages 4 / 2.4 km (wet in places)

Main bodies of water Alfred and Burrows Lakes, Burrows and Kenogami Rivers

Start Ashmore Creek by road (Trans Canada Pipeline Road off Hwy 584)

Finish Longlac by road (Hwy 11)

This route joins Route 32 at Burrows Lake. Signs of past and present logging operations are evident throughout the area.

Low water in July and August may cause difficulties. Fishing: pike, pickerel.

Detailed information *Kenogami Canoe Route No. 2*

Source Ministry of Natural Resources, Box 640, Geraldton, Ontario P0T 1M0

Route (34) Kenogami No. 3

Type Lake and river route

Rating B A C A

Length 55 km / 3 days

Portages 6

Main bodies of water Kenogamisis Lake, Kenogamisis and Kenogami Rivers

Start Kenogamisis Lake by road (Hwy 11)

Finish Longlac by road (Hwy 11)

Portages bypass two old dams, part of a skid road and an old bridge. Cottages are scattered along the shores of Kenogamisis Lake, and canoeists may find heavy boat traffic on the lake.

Low water levels may cause difficulties in July and August. Fishing: pike, pickerel.

Detailed information *Kenogami Canoe Route No. 3*

Source Ministry of Natural Resources, Box 640, Geraldton, Ontario P0T 1M0

Route (35) Steel River Loop

Type River and lake route

Rating A B A A

Length 155 km / 10 to 15 days

Portages 18 / 1.7 km (steep)

Main bodies of water Santoy, Cairngorm and Steel Lakes, Steel River

Start / Finish Santoy Lake by road (off Hwy 17)

Intermediate access Kawabatongog Lake by road (Kimberley-Clark logging road)

Canadian Pacific Railway brochures of the 1890s praised this route to entice people to travel to the area by rail. The route inscribes a long, narrow loop stretching north of Hwy 17, just east of the town of Terrace Bay. The west side of the loop consists mainly of travel on long, narrow lakes and alternates between rugged cliffs and ravines and low, swampy areas with many beaver meadows. A great blue heronry flourishes on the islands of Cairngorm Lake. The route turns around at Aster Lake and heads back south along the Steel River, which features cliffs, some small lakes and a picturesque twenty-metre waterfall. For the last quarter of the route the Steel River winds through a lowland area forming numerous ponds and oxbows. Some canoeists prefer to do only half of this trip. They start at Kawabatongog Lake, fifteen kilometres above the loop, and paddle south to Aster Lake, where they make the choice between the lake or river corridor.

Winds come up quickly on the larger lakes, and caution must be observed. Additional portaging may be necessary during prolonged dry spells. Fishing: pike, pickerel, lake trout, speckled trout.

Route (36) Kagiano River

Type River and lake route

Rating B C B B

Length 52 km / 3 to 4 days

Portages 12

Main bodies of water David, Michael and Solann Lakes, Kagiano River

Start Boat Lake by road (American Can Company Road off Hwy 614)

Finish Lower Landing on the Pic River by logging road

The river sections of this route are almost equally divided between small, swift rapids and slow, meandering flat water. The long, narrow lakes are really just broadenings of the river.

Fishing: pickerel, pike, speckled trout.

Detailed information *Steel River Circle Route*. Canoeists who wish to start at Kawabatongog Lake and travel either the river or lake half of the route should choose one of the following pamphlets:
Steel River Canoe Route or *Steel Lake Canoe Route*.

Source Ministry of Natural Resources,
Box 280, Terrace Bay, Ontario P0T 2W0

Detailed information *Kagiano River Canoe Route*

Source Ministry of Natural Resources,
Box 280, Terrace Bay, Ontario P0T 2W0

Route (37) Foch-Nagagami

Type River route

Rating B B B C

Length 105 km / 4 to 5 days

Portages 11 / 1 km, 2 km

Main bodies of water Foch River, Nagagami Lake, Nagagami River

Start Foch River by rail (VIA)

Finish Hwy 11

Intermediate access Nagagamisis Provincial Park by road (Hwy 631)

The twenty-four-kilometre Foch River section of this route abounds in rapids, shallows and swifts, most of which will pose no problem to the experienced canoeist, though by late summer some walking and lining may be necessary. The canoeist arrives next in Nagagami Lake, where there are several tourist camps; at one time a fur trading post also stood on this lake. The canoeist then joins the Nagagami River, which makes up the bulk of this route. The river offers a mixture of deep, slow-moving sections and violent rapids that must be portaged. The vegetation is generally typical of the boreal forest, chiefly black spruce with some mature jack pine stands, poplars and cedars providing variety.

A side trip can be made into Nagagamisis Lake Provincial Park, near the halfway point. The wind can make both Nagagami and Nagagamisis Lakes treacherous. Fishing: brook trout, pickerel, pike.

Route (38) Upper Missinaibi River

Type River and lake route

Rating B B B A

Length 236 km / 10 to 12 days

Portages 28 / 1.5 km

Main bodies of water Missinaibi Lake, Missinaibi River, Brunswick Lake

Start Missanabie by road (Hwy 651) or rail (VIA)

Finish Mattice by road (Hwy 11)

Intermediate access Missinaibi Lake Provincial Park by road (Wrong Lake Road), Peterbell Lake by rail (VIA)

Many of the portages on this difficult route were blazed by voyageurs and fur company factors more than 200 years ago. For over a century the Missinaibi River remained the Hudson's Bay Company's chief communications and supply line between James Bay and Lake Superior. Much of the travel on Missinaibi Lake is through Missinaibi Lake Provincial Park, and this historic — and potentially hazardous — body of water offers a shoreline dotted with Indian pictographs, old logging camps and the abandoned Hudson's Bay post, Brunswick House. Near Peterbell the river meanders for ten kilometres through the various bog communities of the Peterbell marsh.

The Missinaibi River features numerous sets of violent rapids and waterfalls. Canoeists with considerable whitewater experience may risk running many of the rapids, but on this isolated river the safest route is always the portage trail. Low water levels in August may make some rapids impassable. Missinaibi Lake can become very rough on windy days and requires extreme caution. This route can be extended down the Missinaibi and Moose Rivers to James Bay. (See Route 28.) Fishing: pickerel, pike, lake trout, whitefish.

Detailed information *Foch-Nagagami Canoe Route*

Source Ministry of Natural Resources,
Box 670, Hearst, Ontario P0L 1N0

Detailed information *Missinaibi River Canoe Route (Missanabie to Mattice)*

Source Ministry of Natural Resources,
34 Birch Street, Chapleau, Ontario P0M 1K0

Routes 39 to 75/Areas M to P

Route

39 Shumka to Missanabie	53 Watabeag River
40 The Shoals	54 Misema River and Howard Lake
41 Chapleau-Nemegosenda Loop	55 Larder Lake to Englehart
42 Pishkanogami	56 Englehart River to Lake Timiskaming
43 Wakami Loop	57 Sydney Creek
44 Wakami River	58 Montreal River to Matachewan
45 Sakatawi	59 West Montreal River
46 Mesomikenda-Dividing Lake Loop	60 Lake Timiskaming-Ottawa River
47 Kamiskotia	61 Marten River Loop
48 Tatachikapika	62 Spanish River
49 Upper Mattagami River	63 Elliot Lake to Depot Lake
50 Noble-Nabakwasi	64 Dunlop Lake-Mace Lake Loop
51 Grassy River	65 Ompa-Little Quirke-Semiwite Lakes
52 Mountjoy	*(Continued opposite)*

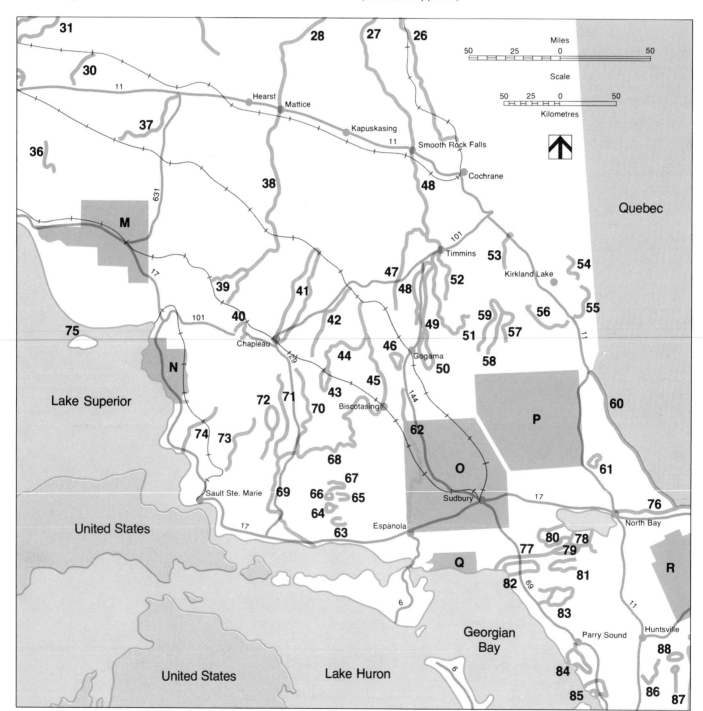

66 Flack Lake-Ten Mile Lake Loop
67 Boland River
68 Upper Mississagi River
69 Lower Mississagi River
70 Wenebegon
71 Aubinadong
72 Ranger Lake Loop
73 Goulais River
74 Batchawana River
75 The Coastal Trip

Area

M White River
N Lake Superior Provincial Park
O Sudbury
P Temagami

Route (39) Shumka to Missanabie

Type Lake and river route

Rating B B B B

Length 80 km / 4 days

Portages 19 / 1 km, 1 km

Main bodies of water Bolkow Lake, Little Missinaibi River, Missinaibi Lake, Baltic Bay, Crooked and Dog Lakes

Start Bolkow Lake by road (off Hwy 651) or rail (VIA)

Finish Missanabie by road (Hwy 651) or rail (VIA)

Intermediate access Missinaibi Lake Provincial Park by road (Wrong Lake Road)

Major geological faults created the long, narrow lakes and fast rivers of this route through the Chapleau Crown Game Preserve. Whitefish Falls is a potentially teacherous highpoint. A variety of bog vegetation flourishes in the marshy lowlands. Indian pictographs mark the rocks along the shore of Missinaibi Lake. Once an important fur trade link between Lake Superior and Missinaibi Lake, this route passes through a region that has been, until recently, a focus of the logging and mining industries. Old logging camps can still be explored. Moose are frequently seen.

Some of the short portages are boggy and difficult to follow. Missinaibi Lake is extremely difficult to navigate in windy weather: wind and waves can easily dash a canoe against the rocky headlands. Some river sections must be lined in late summer. Several side trips into Missinaibi Lake Provincial Park are possible. Fishing: pickerel, northern pike, lake trout, brook trout.

Route (40) The Shoals

Type Lake route

Rating B B C C

Length 56 km / 3 days

Portages 15

Main bodies of water Prairie Bee, Windermere and Little Wawa Lakes

Start Prairie Bee Lake by road (Hwy 101)

Finish Little Wawa Lake by road (Hwy 101)

This route can be broken into two shorter trips, called the North and South Loops. The forty-kilometre, two-day North Loop traverses the large Prairie Bee and Windermere Lakes and ends on Little Wawa Lake. It features remnants of the extensive logging industry that flourished in this area from 1901 to 1956. By 1933 the Austin and Nicholson Lumber Company, based here, was the world's largest producer of railway ties. The company established numerous bush camps to supply the mills of Nicholson on the north shore of Windermere Lake. The houses of this once booming town are now used as summer cottages. The sixteen-kilometre South Loop is a one-day paddle across small lakes through the interior of The Shoals Provincial Park. In a past geological age Lake Sultan covered this area, and glacial sand deposits are present today.

Wind can cause trouble on Prairie Bee and Windermere Lakes. Low water levels in August may make the South Loop impassable. Fishing: pickerel, pike.

Detailed information *Shumka to Missanabie Canoe Route*

Source Ministry of Natural Resources,
34 Birch Street, Chapleau, Ontario P0M 1K0

Detailed information *The Shoals Canoe Route*

Source Ministry of Natural Resources,
34 Birch Street, Chapleau, Ontario P0M 1K0

Route (41) Chapleau-Nemegosenda Loop

Type Lake and river route

Rating B B B A

Length 236 km / 10 to 14 days

Portages 47

Main bodies of water Chapleau Lake, Chapleau River, Henderson, D'Arcy, Schewabik and Kapuskasing Lakes, Nemegosenda River, Nemegosenda Lake, Borden River, Borden Lake

Start / Finish Chapleau by road (Hwy 129) or rail (VIA)

Intermediate access Several points by road

This route follows the Chapleau River downstream through long lakes and turbulent rapids along the eastern boundary of the Chapleau Crown Game Preserve. There is an abundant moose population in this area. The route returns up the Nemegosenda River, which features a variety of bog communities. An Indian graveyard stands on the shore of Frog Lake, and old logging camps and chutes dot the route.

There is a small community at Elsas on Kapuskasing Lake, but no supplies are available at any point on the route. Only two campsites exist between Elsas and Frog Lake, a distance of about forty kilometres. Kapuskasing, Nemegosenda and Borden Lakes can be very rough on windy days. This trip can be extended to James Bay from Elsas via the Kapuskasing, Mattagami and Moose Rivers, adding 500 kilometres and two to three weeks. Fishing: pickerel, pike, brook trout.

Route (42) Pishkanogami

Type River and lake route

Rating B B B B

Length 105 km / 4 days

Portages 15 / 3 km

Main bodies of water Kinogama River, Denyes and Raney Lakes, Ivanhoe River, Ivanhoe Lake

Start Kormak by road (Hwy 667) or rail (VIA)

Finish Foleyet by road (Hwy 101) or rail (VIA)

This route offers a diversity of quiet river, lake and whitewater canoeing. The most dramatic sight is a nine-metre waterfall north of Vice Lake. Pishkanogami means "farther still" and is the Indian name for the Ivanhoe River. Logging, trapping and prospecting orginally opened this route, and logging operations are still evident in the Tooms Lake area. The forty-one-kilometre paddle on Ivanhoe Lake crosses into Ivanhoe Lake Provincial Park, an alternate endpoint for this trip.

Motorboats may be encountered on Ivanhoe Lake. Whitewater experience is recommended for this route. Fishing: pike, pickerel, whitefish.

Detailed information *Chapleau-Nemegosenda Waterway Provincial Park*

Source Ministry of Natural Resources, 34 Birch Street, Chapleau, Ontario P0M 1K0

Detailed information *Pishkanogami Canoe Route*

Source Ministry of Natural Resources, 34 Birch Street, Chapleau, Ontario P0M 1K0

Route (43) Wakami Loop

Type Lake and river route

Rating B B C B

Length 56 km / 3 days

Portages 8

Main bodies of water Wakami and Little Wakami Lakes, Little Wakami and Wakami Rivers

Start / Finish Wakami Lake Provincial Park by road (off Hwy 667)

A logging museum in Wakami Lake Provincial Park may interest canoeists, for old logging roads, lumber camps and a log chute are major attractions along this route. Also of interest are a replica of a trapper's cabin, which stands amid the sugar maples and yellow birch at the north end of Wakami Lake, and the ruins of a Hudson's Bay Company post on the south shore. Ospreys are frequently seen on this lake, and a nesting pair of bald eagles has been reported. Rare orchids can also be found.

Wakami Lake can be extremely rough on windy days. Fishing: pickerel, pike.

Detailed information *Wakami Loop Canoe Route*

Source Ministry of Natural Resources,
34 Birch Street, Chapleau, Ontario P0M 1K0

Route (44) Wakami River

Type River and lake route

Rating B B B B

Length 124 km / 5 to 7 days

Portages 35 / 540 m (rough terrain)

Main bodies of water Wakami Lake, Wakami River, Ridout, Ransom and Bayly Lakes, Woman River, Horwood Lake

Start Wakami Lake Provincial Park by road (off Hwy 667), Sultan by road (Hwy 667 or Eddy Forest Agreement Road) or rail (VIA)

Finish Horwood Lake by road (off Hwy 616) or Groundhog River by rail (VIA)

Intermediate access Logging roads

The Wakami is a fast-flowing river with many boulder-strewn rapids. Turbulent waterfalls are frequent, and an especially impressive — and dangerous — series of falls marks the flow of the Woman River into Horwood Lake. Part of this route once served as a Hudson's Bay Company supply line, and logging chutes and bridges, as well as two abandoned gold mines in the vicinity, are evidence of other past uses of the area.

From early spring into June the Wakami River boils with treacherous white water, but in August the water level is often so low that rocky shallows must be walked down. This route can be extended via the Groundhog, Mattagami and Moose Rivers to Moosonee, adding 500 kilometres and two to three weeks. Fishing: pike, pickerel, whitefish, brook trout.

Detailed information *Wakami River Canoe Route*

Source Ministry of Natural Resources,
34 Birch Street, Chapleau, Ontario P0M 1K0

Route (45) Sakatawi

Type Lake and river route

Rating B B B B

Length 120 km / 5 days

Portages 14 / 2.4 km

Main bodies of water Biscotasi, Opeepeesway and Rush Lakes, Rush and Woman Rivers, Horwood Lake

Start Biscotasing by road (off Hwy 667 or off Hwy 144) or rail (VIA)

Finish Horwood Lake by road (off Hwy 616) or Groundhog River by rail (VIA)

Intermediate access Biscotasi Lake can be skipped at the beginning by taking the Eddy Forest Agreement Road to the head of Biscotasi Creek.

This historic route has been used for hundreds of years by native peoples and, during the fur trade era, by the Hudson's Bay Company. Old logging roads and camps, three abandoned gold mines and the ghost town of Jerome, on the south shore of Opeepeesway Lake, can be seen along the way. In addition to travel on large lakes, this route crosses smaller lakes and follows winding rivers. The rapids along these rivers are often impressive and violent, especially where the Woman River plunges into Horwood Lake. Moose are a common sight, and wolf, lynx and bear also inhabit the area.

The large lakes must be navigated with care during windy weather. This route can be extended down the Groundhog, Mattagami and Moose Rivers to James Bay, adding 500 kilometres and two to three weeks. Fishing: pickerel, whitefish; brook trout in some feeder streams.

Route (46) Mesomikenda-Dividing Lake Loop

Type Lake route

Rating C C B B

Length 61 km / 3 to 4 days

Portages 13

Main bodies of water Mesomikenda, Somme, Three Duck and Dividing Lakes

Start / Finish Mesomikenda Lake campground by road (off Hwy 144)

Except for a few cottages on Mesomikenda Lake, this route links a chain of uninhabited lakes in a typical northern bush landscape. Some rapids occur in the short river stretches connecting the lakes, and many good campsites dot the lake shores. Sand beaches offer good swimming at several points along the route, and Schist Lake, named for its schist rock outcrops, contains numerous islands and bays.

A slow-moving current makes it possible to canoe this route either upstream or downstream. The stretch below Lower Three Duck Lake is very difficult to navigate, and the canoe may have to be lined down. Fishing: pike, pickerel.

Detailed information *Sakatawi Canoe Route*

Source Ministry of Natural Resources, 34 Birch Street, Chapleau, Ontario P0M 1K0

Detailed information *Mesomikenda-Dividing Lake Loop*

Source Ministry of Natural Resources, Box 129, Gogama, Ontario P0M 1W0

Route (47) Kamiskotia

Type River and lake route

Rating B B B B

Length 131 km / 7 days

Portages 32 / 1 km, 2 km, 1 km

Main bodies of water Kenogaming, Akweskwa and Opishing Lakes, Kamiskotia and Mattagami Rivers

Start Kenogaming Lake by road (Kenogaming Lake Road off Hwy 144 at Gogama)

Finish Timmins by road (Hwy 101) or rail (Ontario Northland)

Intermediate access Hwy 101 between Beaucage and Opishing Lakes, logging roads in Whitesides, Massey and Robb Townships

Flowing through an uninhabited area of spruce forest, this route starts out on lakes and passes into a long and winding stretch of river canoeing, where frequent rapids offer a challenge to the experienced canoeist. Used for thousands of years by nomadic Indian families travelling to winter hunting and trapping grounds, this waterway became important to prospectors and surveyors when gold was discovered in Porcupine in 1908. By the late 1940s forest access roads began to reach the Kamiskotia River and were used to transport virgin timber. Because of these roads, the Kamiskotia was one of the few rivers in the area to escape the log drives, and most of its rapids and trout pools are in a comparatively natural state.

At least eleven of the portages must be carried over under all circumstances. Many other rapids can only be run at high water levels. On the central portion of the route water levels over rapids may be reduced to a mere trickle by late July. Because of seepage from mine tailings along the last portion of the Kamiskotia River, drinking water should be drawn only from feeder streams on the north shore. Fishing: pike, pickerel; brook trout in feeder streams and rapids.

Route (48) Tatachikapika

Type River route

Rating B C B C

Length 95 km / 4 to 5 days

Portages 17 / 1.4 km, 1.4 km, 1 km

Main bodies of water Tatachikapika Lake, Tatachikapika and Mattagami Rivers

Start Tatachikapika Lake by road (Roblin Township road off Hwy 144)

Finish Timmins by road (Hwy 101) or rail (Ontario Northland)

Intermediate access Hwy 144, Tatachikapika Lodge Road, logging roads

The original portages along this route were blazed in the late 1700s by native families trading at two Hudson's Bay Company posts in the area. Many old clearings with remnants of early logging camps are reminders of the area's more recent past. For the first third of the trip the Tatachikapika is a narrow river, winding through a wide valley bordered by sand and gravel ridges with occasional rock outcroppings. The shoreline tends to be swampy here, but gradually becomes defined farther downstream as the river runs wider with increasingly straight stretches. At other points there are very shallow stretches of rapids, some three kilometres long, with no portages.

The section of the Tatachikapika River between Hwy 144 and the Mattagami River is suited to canoeing only during the high-water period between breakup in mid May and the first week in June. This stretch should never be run by novices, who should end their trip at Hwy 144. Fishing: pike, pickerel, limited brook trout.

Detailed information *Kamiskotia Canoe Route*

Source Ministry of Natural Resources, 896 Riverside Drive, Timmins, Ontario P4N 3W2

Detailed information *Tatachikapika Canoe Route*

Source Ministry of Natural Resources, 896 Riverside Drive, Timmins, Ontario P4N 3W2

Route (49) Upper Mattagami River

Type River and lake route

Rating B A B B

Length 210 km / 8 days

Portages 10 / 1.6 km

Main bodies of water Minisinakwa, Mattagami and Kenogamissi Lakes, Mattagami River

Start Gogama by road (Hwy 661) or rail (VIA)

Finish Railroad bridge south of Smooth Rock Falls. There is road access to the Falls.

Intermediate access Mattagami and Kenogamissi Lakes by road (Hwy 144), Timmins by road (Hwy 101)

The Gogama-Timmins half of this route follows a series of long, narrow lakes, touching on the Mattagami Indian Reserve near the mouth of the Minisinakwa River. The village stands on a point covered with red pine, trees saved by Indian fire fighters during the 1941 Gogama forest fire, which ravaged 132 000 hectares of surrounding timber. Farther along this section of the route are the ruins of a Hudson's Bay Company post on Mattagami Lake and a plaque on the west shore of Kenogamissi Lake marking the site of an early fur trade post. Below Timmins the Mattagami River runs through both farm land and more remote areas. Rapids along this stretch require additional canoeing experience. The deep-flowing Mattagami is a clay-banked river. This clay can be a nuisance clinging to the canoeist's shoes, but it also provides fertile ground for the lush vegetation growing along the shore. Raspberries, currants, gooseberries, blueberries and cranberries flourish in season. The clay bank also carries the tracks of local animal life, including wolf, bear, moose, fox and mink. Once an important fur trade link, the Mattagami River became a significant source of transport and power generation after the 1908 discovery of gold at Timmins. Much of the land along this route has been staked for mining claims. From the 1930s to the present the Abitibi Pulp and Paper Company has maintained an intensive woodcutting operation along the river. Below the excellent campsite at Island Falls (about twenty kilometres south of Smooth Rock Falls) cottages and fishermen are common.

The last five kilometres of Kenogamissi Lake to Wawaitin Falls is wide and shallow and should be avoided in windy weather. Below Timmins drinking water must be treated. Fishing: pickerel, pike.

Detailed information *Mattagami River Canoe Route (Gogama to Smooth Rock Falls)*

Source Ministry of Natural Resources,
Box 129, Gogama, Ontario P0M 1W0
or
Ministry of Natural Resources,
896 Riverside Drive, Timmins, Ontario P4N 3W2

Route (50) Noble-Nabakwasi

Type River and lake route

Rating C C C C

Length 52 km / 3 days

Portages 8

Main bodies of water Minisinakwa Lake, Noble River, Groves, Hanover and Londonderry Lakes, Donnegana, Nabakwasi and Minisinakwa Rivers

Start Gogama by road (Hwy 144) or rail (VIA)

Finish Picnic grounds on Minisinakwa River by road (off Hwy 144)

This short, straightforward route never wanders far from population centres and is a good choice for beginners. One long set of rapids and two scenic waterfalls are bypassed on the last portage.

Fishing: pike, pickerel.

Detailed information *Noble-Nabakwasi Canoe Route*

Source Ministry of Natural Resources,
Box 129, Gogama, Ontario P0M 1W0

Route (51) Grassy River

Type Lake and river route

Rating B A B B

Length 165 km / 8 days

Portages 4 / 2 km, 1.4 km

Main bodies of water Halliday, Canoeshed, Grassy, Kapiskong and Peterlong Lakes, Grassy River

Start Halliday Lake by road (off Hwy 560) or Canoeshed Lake by road (off Hwy 566)

Finish Timmins by road (Hwy 101) or rail (Ontario Northland)

Intermediate access Several roads in the area

From the headwater lake, Halliday, through to Grassy Lake, the Grassy River forms many oxbows and braided channels as it passes through a wide variety of marshlands with little appreciable drop. This area provides excellent opportunities to view wildfowl and big game. From Grassy Lake to the dam on Peterlong Lake the landscape changes from deep peats and glacial deposits to shallow-soiled, open bedrock. Below the dam the Grassy River breaks into rapids and swifts, and at High Falls it plunges into a deep gorge, which continues for twenty kilometres to the Mattagami River north of Timmins. Once an important source of raw fur for both the Hudson's Bay Company and the North West Company, the Grassy River system still supports extensive trapping. The route is also rich in relics of the timber and mining industries.

The first section of this route can be turned into a circular lake trip with short portages. The portage above High Falls must be approached with extreme caution. Water levels below High Falls are generally shallow after late June. Fishing: pickerel, pike; brook trout below High Falls.

Route (52) Mountjoy

Type Lake and river route

Rating C B B C

Length 72 km / 4 days

Portages 13 / 1.4 km

Main bodies of water Muskasenda and Papakomeka Lakes, Mountjoy River

Start Muskasenda Lake by road (Papakomeka Lake Road)

Finish Timmins by road (Hwy 101) or rail (Ontario Northland)

Intermediate access Papakomeka Lake Road

An excellent waterway for group or family canoeing, the Mountjoy River system was the primary route for prospectors, miners and loggers before the construction of roads in the area. Two local gold mines produced combined total revenue exceeding $2 300 000 between 1926 and 1964, when gold sold under $35 an ounce. Rich deposits may still lie undiscovered in the river basin. Many rock outcroppings along this route show signs of early trenching and blasting by prospectors. From 1910 to 1960 the river was used to drive logs to sawmills in Timmins. In the off-season many of the loggers, mainly Norwegian and Finnish, cleared homestead farms on or near the river. Today, only small, overgrown clearings mark these locations. The area between Marceau and Papakomeka Lakes is heavily used by cottagers, fishermen and boaters.

Water flows deeply over rapids only from breakup to early June. The first seven portages must be carried at all times; the last six may be run in early spring by those with moderate to good whitewater skills. Fishing: pike, pickerel, perch; brook trout in large rapids and feeder streams; lake trout in Muskasenda Lake.

Detailed information *Grassy River Canoe Route*

Source Ministry of Natural Resources,
896 Riverside Drive, Timmins, Ontario P4N 3W2

Detailed information *Mountjoy Canoe Route*

Source Ministry of Natural Resources,
896 Riverside Drive, Timmins, Ontario P4N 3W2

Route (53) Watabeag River

Type River route

Rating A n/a C B

Length 39 km / 3 days

Portages 7

Main body of water Watabeag River

Start Sylvia Falls by road (Watabeag Lake Road off Hwy 11)

Finish Matheson by road (Hwy 11)

Several rapids on the Watabeag River provide an excellent introduction to fast water for the beginner. Used extensively in the 1940s and 1950s for log drives, the river flows through some agricultural settlement on the Great Clay Belt at its extreme northern end and through forested areas for the rest of its length.

Low water in late summer may require lining canoes over a four- to eight-kilometre stretch below Egan Chutes. Fast water and rapids make this route hazardous in periods of high water. Drinking water should be treated. Fishing: brook trout, pike, pickerel.

Route (54) Misema River and Howard Lake

Type Lake route

Rating C B C B

Length 39 km / 2 days

Portages 4

Main bodies of water Beaverhouse, Misema, Howard, Kennedy, Verna, Keith, Marten and Rat Lakes

Start / Finish Beaverhouse Lake by road (Upper Beaver Mine Road off Hwy 66)

Intermediate access Howard Lake by road (Esker Lakes Road off Hwy 66)

This route begins on Beaverhouse Lake and winds north through a chain of good fishing lakes; it then turns and follows these same lakes back to the starting point. The rocky shorelines are broken by numerous bays and points, some with sandy beaches. Rich in native history, the region offers prehistoric pictographs on Misema Lake, an Indian graveyard on Verna Lake and one of the oldest Indian villages in the area on Beaverhouse Lake. The southern portion of this route features extensive rock outcroppings, and the west side of the waterway coincides approximately with the eastern limit of the Munro Esker. Human habitation is limited to scattered cottages and the small Indian settlement on Beaverhouse Lake.

A shallow spill dam between Beaverhouse Lake and the Misema River maintains the water level throughout the canoeing season. Drinking water should be treated and may require settling. This route can be extended eastward from Kinabik Lake to Labyrinth Lake or from Marten Lake to the Magusi River or westward from Rat Lake to Esker Lakes Provincial Park. Fishing: pickerel, pike, smallmouth bass.

Detailed information *Watabeag River Canoe Route (Sylvia Falls to Matheson)*

Source Ministry of Natural Resources, Box 129, Swastika, Ontario P0K 1T0

Detailed information *Misema River and Howard Lake Route*

Source Ministry of Natural Resources, Box 129, Swastika, Ontario, P0K 1T0

Route (55) Larder Lake to Englehart

Type Lake and river route

Rating B B C B

Length 64 km / 3 days

Portages 10

Main bodies of water Larder, Raven, Corset, Ward, Skead, Skeleton and Wendigo Lakes, Larder River

Start Raven Lake by road (off Hwy 66), town of Larder Lake by road (Hwy 66)

Finish Wendigo Lake by road (off Hwy 569 or off Hwy 624)

Laurel and Abitibi Indians used this waterway; it was also a secondary route from Montreal to Abitibi Lake during the fur trade era. In more recent times gold brought many prospectors into the area, which was to become one of Canada's gold-mining centres. This route provided the main traffic artery for mining exploration and for the development of Larder Lake Camp from 1901 to 1906. Today, despite logging on both sides of the route and cottages on Raven and Wendigo Lakes, most of the waterway has been preserved in its natural state. The route traverses twelve scenic lakes, with plenty of fast water and several sets of rapids and falls. The shoreline is banked by high rocky bluffs and stands of red and white pine.

This route should be avoided during spring runoff and other periods of high water. Larder Lake can be extremely dangerous in high winds. Some rapids can be run by experienced canoeists, but use of all portages is recommended. Drinking water should be treated. This route can be extended from Englehart for twenty-eight kilometres down the Blanche River to Lake Timiskaming. (See Route 56.) Fishing: northern pike, pickerel, brook trout, lake trout, smallmouth bass.

Route (56) Englehart River to Lake Timiskaming

Type River and lake route

Rating A B B B

Length 120 km / 5 days

Portages 11

Main bodies of water Englehart River, Kushog, Kinogami and Robillard Lakes, Blanche River

Start Englehart River by road (E.M.U. Road off Hwy 66)

Finish Judge by road (Hwy 65)

This waterway was a major access route for settlers and lumbermen in the late nineteenth and early twentieth centuries, and steamboats once plied the navigable portions of the Blanche River between New Liskeard and Englehart. The route starts in forested areas, but soon makes its way into the farming country of the Little Clay Belt, where several communities were destroyed in the disastrous 1922 Haileybury forest fire. Because the route frequently travels through a deep, heavily forested valley, it seems farther from civilization than it actually is. Three villages, five commercial resorts and cottages are found along the way. Dangerous rapids churn over rock outcroppings on the most scenic part of the trip, and the most impressive waterfall is High Falls in Kap-Kig-Iwan Provincial Park.

The stretch from Charlton to the Blanche River should be avoided during spring runoff and other periods of high water. In the agricultural area water should be treated. Most of the land along the route is privately owned, and permission must be requested before camping. Fishing: pickerel, pike, smallmouth bass, brook trout, sturgeon.

Detailed information *Larder Lake to Englehart*

Source Ministry of Natural Resources, Box 129, Swastika, Ontario P0K 1T0

Detailed information *Englehart River to Lake Timiskaming*

Source Ministry of Natural Resources, Box 129, Swastika, Ontario P0K 1T0

Route (57) Sydney Creek

Type Lake and river route

Rating C C C B

Length 32 km / 2 days

Portages 7

Main bodies of water Longpoint, Shillington and Sydney Lakes

Start Longpoint Lake by road (Hwy 560)

Finish Sydney Lake by road (off Hwy 65)

This route follows a series of small, scenic lakes that provided access for mining exploration in the early 1900s. Many ridges and bluffs of the Canadian Shield parallel the waterway. Except for one resort and a few cottages on Longpoint Lake, the area is uninhabited. Bear and moose may be sighted.

Drinking water should be treated. Fishing: pickerel, pike, smallmouth bass.

Detailed information *Gowganda to Matachewan Routes*. The Sydney Creek route can be combined with either of the other two routes described in this brochure: the West Montreal River (Wapus Creek to Matachewan) for an extra seventy-six kilometres and three days or the Montreal River (Edith Lake to Matachewan) for an extra fifty-two kilometres and two to three days.

Source Ministry of Natural Resources,
Box 129, Swastika, Ontario P0K 1T0

Route (58) Montreal River to Matachewan

Type Lake and river route

Rating C B B B

Length 40 km / 2 to 3 days

Portages 15 / 1.8 km

Main bodies of water Stumpy, Gowganda, Burk, Edith, Obushkong, Crotch, Tommy and Sisseney Lakes; Montreal River

Start Edith Lake by road (off Hwy 560)

Finish Matachewan by road (Hwy 66)

The Gowganda silver rush of 1907 brought prospectors across these lakes, and there is still some evidence of their old trenches along the portages. The area was also logged over in the early 1900s, and remnants of old log chutes and dams can be seen at several points.

Drinking water should be treated. Fishing: pickerel, pike, smallmouth bass.

Detailed information *Gowganda to Matachewan Routes*. The Montreal River to Matachewan route can be combined with either of the other two routes described in this brochure: the West Montreal River (Wapus Creek to Matachewan) for an extra sixty-four kilometres and three days or Sydney Creek (Longpoint Lake to Sydney Lake) for an extra forty-five kilometres and two days. It can also be extended down the Montreal River an extra twenty kilometres to Elk Lake.

Source Ministry of Natural Resources,
Box 129, Swastika, Ontario P0K 1T0

Route (59) West Montreal River

Type Lake and river route

Rating C B B B

Length 64 km / 3 days

Portages 8

Main bodies of water Metikemedo, Penassi, Mistinikon, Rankin and Matachewan Lakes, West Montreal River

Start Wapus Creek by road (Hwy 560)

Finish Matachewan by road (Hwy 66)

This route follows a series of linear lakes that are really widenings of the West Montreal River. An excellent beach on Rankin Lake and several duck nesting areas are highlights of this relatively easy wilderness trip. Only scant evidence remains of Fort Matachewan, a Hudson's Bay post that operated on Lower Matachewan Lake from 1865 to 1920.

A control dam at Matachewan Falls and Upper Notch Dam, between Duncan and Metikemedo Lakes, can affect water levels. Drinking water should be treated. Fishing: pickerel, pike, lake trout.

Detailed information *Gowganda to Matachewan Routes*. The West Montreal River route can be combined with either of the other two routes described in this brochure: the Montreal River (Edith Lake to Matachewan) for an extra forty kilometres and two days or Sydney Creek (Longpoint Lake to Sydney Lake) for an extra forty-five kilometres and two days. It can also be extended down the Montreal River an extra twenty kilometres to Elk Lake.

Source Ministry of Natural Resources, Box 129, Swastika, Ontario P0K 1T0

Route (60) Lake Timiskaming-Ottawa River

Type Lake and river route

Rating C C C B

Length 226 km / 10 to 13 days

Portages 2 / 1 km

Main bodies of water Lake Timiskaming, Ottawa River

Start Haileybury by road (Hwy 558 or 11B)

Finish Driftwood Provincial Park by road (Hwy 17)

Intermediate access Several points by road along Quebec Hwy 101 and Ontario Hwys 63, 533 and 17

Flowing between Ontario and Quebec, the waters of Lake Timiskaming and the Ottawa River cut through a large, continuous valley with steep, tree-covered hills and cliffs on both sides. Near the beginning of the trip Devil Rock, a sheer 150-metre cliff, drops into Lake Timiskaming, one of the deepest lakes in Ontario. Several historic sites dot the course of this route, including the site of Fort Temiscaming, a long-time Catholic mission and Hudson's Bay post. Near the fifty-kilometre mark the wild and beautiful Kipawa River is located on the Quebec shore. A walk up this river on the north shore brings the traveller to the impressive waterfall called *Grande Chute*, one of the most scenic attractions on Lake Timiskaming. Approximately 100 kilometres into the trip a dam marks the boundary between the lake and the Ottawa River. Several hydro-electric dams along this route have flooded kilometres of rapids, including the treacherous stretch of Long Sault Rapids, south of Timiskaming and Thorne. Further on, the Mattawa River flows into the Ottawa River, and an interesting side trip can be taken a few kilometres upstream to Samuel de Champlain Provincial Park, where camping and road access are available. Another seventy kilometres brings the canoeist to Driftwood Provincial Park, the usual endpoint of this trip. Ten kilometres beyond the park is the Des Joachims Dam, the largest on the Upper Ottawa River. Downstream from the dam is Deep River Canyon, one of the few remaining "valleys" caused by faulting. Here a plateau of naked granite juts 210 metres above the valley floor, just as it did when the glacier scarred it.

Lake Timiskaming can be extremely dangerous in windy weather. Extra caution should be used close to all dams. Campsites are limited on the lake but numerous along the Ottawa River. Drinking water should be treated. Fishing: pickerel, pike, lake trout, bass, perch, muskellunge.

Detailed information *Lake Timiskaming-Ottawa River Route*

Source Ministry of Natural Resources, Box 3070, 222 McIntyre Street West, North Bay, Ontario P1B 8K7

Route (61) Marten River Loop

Type Lake and river route

Rating C B B C

Length 35 km / 2 to 3 days

Portages 2 / 2.5 km

Main bodies of water Marten River, Wicksteed, Bruce, Big Marten and Little Marten Lakes

Start / Finish Marten River Provincial Park by road (Hwy 11 or 64)

Intermediate access Little Marten Lake by road (off Hwy 11), Wicksteed Lake Dam by road (off Hwy 11)

An ideal circle route for campers staying at Marten River Provincial Park, this trip offers good opportunities for fishing and wildlife viewing. Also of interest is the logging exhibition in the park. J.R. Booth, the "Ottawa Valley Lumber Baron", established a logging camp on Wicksteed Lake in 1905. Since that time several other companies have cut in the surrounding bush. Many massive stumps are scattered throughout the young pine, birch and maple forest common to this area. Wicksteed Lake is uninhabited, and its numerous islands and bays provide scenic spots for camping or a day of exploring. The long portage trail out of Wicksteed Lake ends at an old lumber camp clearing on Bruce Lake. Remnants of turn-of-the-century logging equipment are still evident along the northern shore of Bruce Lake. Most of this route travels within the Nipissing Crown Game Preserve, and moose are a common sight.

The one long portage between Wicksteed and Bruce Lakes should be attempted only by strong, experienced canoeists. A less strenuous trip is possible by returning directly from Wicksteed Lake and then setting out again through Little Marten and Big Marten Lakes to Bruce Lake. The lakes can be hazardous on windy days. Fishing: pike, pickerel, lake trout.

Route (62) Spanish River

Type River route

Rating B C B C

Length 190 km / 10 days

Portages 12 / 2 km, 1.6 km

Main bodies of water Duke Lake, Spanish River, Agnew Lake

Start Duke Lake by road (Duke Lake Road off Hwy 144)

Finish Agnew Lake by road (off Hwy 17 at Webbwood)

Intermediate access By logging roads or rail (VIA)

An abundance of fast water and rapids makes this route a solid choice for the moderately experienced whitewater enthusiast. The Spanish River links a series of narrow, numbered lakes — Tenth to First — with a varied shoreline of poplar and birch, jack and red pine, reedy bays, rocky cliffs and sandy beaches. Numerous campsites dot the route, and human settlement is minimal. The ruins of two old logging camps lie just above the hazardous Graveyard Rapids, which have claimed several lives. These rapids can be portaged either in one long trek or in six shorter moves. Once past the Graveyard and the rapids at the mouth of the Agnes River, this route offers excellent downstream canoeing, with fast-flowing water and navigable rapids all the way to Agnew Lake.

Many of the rapids can be run, but some, such as the Graveyard, must be portaged by everyone travelling the river. At Agnew Lake Lodge transportation can be arranged to Webbwood for a minimal fee. The trip can be extended to the north shore of Georgian Bay, but below Espanola the Spanish River is polluted. Fishing: pike, pickerel.

Detailed information *Marten River Canoe Route*

Source Ministry of Natural Resources, Box 3070, 222 McIntyre Street West, North Bay, Ontario P1B 8K7

Detailed information *Spanish River Canoe Route* (*Duke Lake to Agnew Lake*)

Source Ministry of Natural Resources, Box 129, Gogama, Ontario P0M 1W0

Route (63) Elliot Lake to Depot Lake

Type Lake route

Rating C B C C

Length 32 km / 3 days

Portages 7

Main bodies of water Elliot, Quimby, Esten, Marshland, Grandeur, Trout and Depot Lakes

Start Elliot Lake by road (Hwy 108)

Finish Depot Lake by road (Hwy 108)

Intermediate access Esten Lake by road (off Hwy 108)

This chain of lakes, with short stretches of river travel, makes an excellent route for the novice canoeist. In the early 1900s this area was extensively logged, and remnants of the logging era can be seen at the first portage. In the 1950s the area was prospected for uranium, which led to the development of Elliot Lake, the only settlement of note on the route. The forest is predominantly pine and birch. Moose may be sighted in marshy areas, and numerous species of waterfowl frequent these waters in the autumn. A small waterfall at the outlet from Elliot Lake to Quimby Lake and a rocky gorge between Esten and Marshland Lakes are scenic attractions.

Three additional portages may be required in August. Larger lakes can become rough in windy weather. Water should not be drunk in large quantities because of seepage from radioactive mine tailings. Fishing: lake trout, whitefish, rock bass.

Route (64) Dunlop Lake-Mace Lake Loop

Type Lake route

Rating n/a B B B

Length 42 km / 3 to 5 days

Portages 9 / 1.4 km

Main bodies of water Dunlop, Ten Mile, Ezma, Upper Mace and Lower Mace Lakes

Start / Finish Dunlop Lake by road (Hwy 108)

Travelling within Mississagi Provincial Park, this route circles a chain of lakes surrounded by hardwood and coniferous forest. Waterfalls on the north shore of Ten Mile Lake, the deepest inland lake in the area, and the islands and sand beach of Upper Mace Lake are special attractions. Moose and black bear live in the area. A choice of side trips can be added to the basic route. There are some cottages on Ten Mile and Dunlop Lakes, but most of the trip passes through untouched wilderness.

Dunlop and Ten Mile Lakes can become very rough in windy weather. Fishing: (spring) lake trout, splake, brook trout; (summer) pickerel, smallmouth bass.

Detailed information *Elliot Lake to Depot Lake Canoe Route*

Source Ministry of Natural Resources, Box 190, 62 Queen Street, Blind River, Ontario P0R 1B0

Detailed information *Dunlop Lake-Mace Lake Canoe Route*

Source Ministry of Natural Resources, Box 190, 62 Queen Street, Blind River, Ontario P0R 1B0

Route (65) Ompa-Little Quirke-Semiwite Lakes

Type Lake route

Rating C C B C

Length 15 km / 1 day

Portages 12 / 1.3 km, 1.2 km

Main bodies of water Ompa and Semiwite Lakes

Start Ompa Lake by road (Hwy 639)

Finish Semiwite Lake by road (Hwy 639)

Lake, pond and stream travel make up this ideal beginners route. The trip can be almost doubled by a side trip to Little Quirke Lake. During the early 1900s a flourishing logging industry cut the large stands of virgin white and red pine, and today the area has regenerated into a predominantly hardwood forest. Remnants of the old logging days can be found along the route. Moose, deer and beaver may also be sighted. Settlement is limited to the Mississagi Provincial Park campgrounds at the west end of Semiwite Lake.

Extensive beaver activity may cause water levels in streams and ponds to fluctuate. Fishing: lake trout, brook trout, rainbow trout.

Route (66) Flack Lake-Ten Mile Lake Loop

Type Lake route

Rating n/a B B B

Length 32 km / 4 days

Portages 13 / 1.1 km, 1.1 km

Main bodies of water Flack, Astonish, Ezma, Ten Mile, Dollyberry, Gibberry, Bobowash and Samreid Lakes

Start / Finish Flack Lake by road (off Hwy 639)

Beginning and ending within Mississagi Provincial Park, this route turns at Ten Mile Lake, the deepest inland lake in the area, with depths in excess of 100 metres. The area is situated in a high section of the Laurentian Plateau, and at the west end of Flack Lake a large hill of quartzite rises 200 metres above lake level. Logged over at the turn of the century, this area also saw exploratory uranium drilling during the 1950s. Ruins of an old logging camp stand near the narrows of Bruce Lake, and an abandoned drill camp can be seen between Olympus and Astonish Lakes. Moose, black bear, beaver and otter inhabit the area. Scattered cottages on Ten Mile Lake are the only settlement.

Flack and Ten Mile Lake can become very rough in windy weather. Fishing is prohibited on one section of this route because of lake trout breeding. Fishing: lake trout, brook trout, whitefish.

Detailed information *Ompa, Little Quirke, Semiwite Lakes Canoe Route*

Source Ministry of Natural Resources, Box 190, 62 Queen Street, Blind River, Ontario P0R 1B0

Detailed information *Flack Lake-Ten Mile Lake Canoe Route*

Source Ministry of Natural Resources, Box 190, 62 Queen Street, Blind River, Ontario P0R 1B0

Route (67) Boland River

Type River and lake route

Rating C B B B

Length 55 km / 4 days

Portages 6 / 1.9 km

Main bodies of water Mount, Rottier, Grey Trout, Rawhide and Little Sister Lakes, Boland River

Start Mount Lake by road (Hwy 546)

Finish Boland River Bridge by road (Hwy 639)

The Boland River area provided rich stands of red and white pine for the logging industry at the turn of the century. Some of this virgin timber still towers on the north shore of Rawhide Lake, and a large stand of virgin jack pine parallels the south bank of the Boland River approximately midway downstream. High cliffs with talus slopes are also an attraction on Rawhide Lake. Moose, black bear and osprey may be sighted at various points along this route. Recent logging has occurred on the north side of the meandering Boland River, and some log jams will be encountered. Other signs of human habitation are limited to a handful of cabins and lodges.

Rawhide Lake can become rough in windy weather. Campsites are abundant along the river, and several are located on the lakes. Fishing: pike, bass, lake trout, brook trout.

Detailed information *Boland River Canoe Route*

Source Ministry of Natural Resources, Box 190, 62 Queen Street, Blind River, Ontario P0R 1B0

Route (68) Upper Mississagi River

Type Lake and river route

Rating B B B B

Length 175 km / 7 to 8 days

Portages 26 / 1.6 km, 1.2 km

Main bodies of water Biscotasi, Ramsey, Spanish, Bardney and Upper Green Lakes, Mississagi River, Rocky Island and Aubrey Lakes

Start Biscotasing by road (off Hwy 667 or off Hwy 144)

Finish Aubrey Falls by road (Hwy 129)

Intermediate access A few logging roads

Once a favourite of the famous woodsman and writer, Grey Owl, this route is now a Waterway Provincial Park. The route begins primarily as lake travel, with stands of massive white pine and an abandoned Hudson's Bay Company post on Upper Green Lake as main points of interest. At the end of Bardney Lake the portage crosses the height of land between the Great Lakes-St. Lawrence and Arctic Watersheds. Farther on, the route features more river travel as the Mississagi makes its way between high hills and jack pine flats. The river sections present great variety, sometimes deep and meandering, sometimes breaking into swifts and rapids. Hellsgate Rapids is particularly impressive, and at Aubrey Falls the water drops over a sheer rock face. Along the lower sections of this route signs of the great 1948 Mississagi forest fire are still evident.

Winds can make the lakes treacherous, and dams often alter water levels. Dangerous rapids and waterfalls and a deceptively fast current are hazards on the fifty-kilometre stretch from Bark Lake to Rocky Island Lake. This route can be extended down the Mississagi River to Lake Huron. (See Route 69.) Fishing: pike, pickerel, lake trout.

Detailed information *Mississagi Canoe Route (Biscotasing to Aubrey Falls)*

Source Ministry of Natural Resources, Box 190, 62 Queen Street, Blind River, Ontario P0R 1B0

Route (69) Lower Mississagi River

Type River route

Rating B B C C

Length 145 km / 5 to 7 days

Portages 6

Main bodies of water Mississagi River, Tunnel and Red Rock Lakes, Lake Huron

Start Aubrey Falls by road (Hwy 129)

Finish Blind River by road (Hwy 17)

Intermediate access The river runs parallel to Hwy 129 or 17 for most of the route.

The Mississagi River provided an important transportation artery for generations of Indians and for the fur traders. During the early 1900s it was used for log drives to the mill in Blind River, and today the river powers three hydro-electric generating stations. Good whitewater stretches such as "Forty Mile" Rapids and scenic spots such as Aubrey Falls offer variety along the way. As one travels downstream, the riverbanks change from sixty-metre cliffs to low shores of sand, gravel and boulders. A mixed forest has replaced the extensive stands of white pine that were logged here at the turn of the century. Moose and black bear are common. Settlement includes the town of Iron Bridge and the Indian reserve at the mouth of the river.

Generating stations can cause the water level to fluctuate as much as two metres; check beforehand with the Ministry of Natural Resources office in Blind River. Some rapids can be run only when the water level is high. Fishing: pickerel, sturgeon, brook trout.

Route (70) Wenebegon

Type River and lake route

Rating B B C B

Length 105 km / 5 days

Portages 16

Main bodies of water Wenebegon Lake, Wenebegon River, Aubrey Lake

Start Burying Creek by road (Hwy 129)

Finish Aubrey Falls by road (Hwy 129)

Intermediate access The river runs roughly parallel to Hwy 129 and is never more than 13 km from it.

The Wenebegon River flows out of Wenebegon Lake and through alder thickets and jack pine forest, with numerous marshy clearings. The surrounding wilderness ranges from lowlands to rolling hills and high rocky bluffs. Much of the route passes through areas burned over in the huge 1948 Mississagi fire. Although some isolated stands of virgin timber survived the blaze, in most places barren, bleached tree trunks tower over the regenerated pines. Many log jams, also left by the fire, crowd parts of the river and lakes. Some are so extensive that a portage is required. Several stretches of rapids offer a whitewater challenge to experienced canoeists, but an alternate route down Seven Mile Bay of Rocky Island Lake will bypass some of the white water along the lower stretches of the Wenebegon River.

Wenebegon Lake is impossible to canoe in windy weather, and canoeists may be wind-bound for a day or more. The Wenebegon River is often extremely low in August. The trip can be ended above the turbulent rapids flowing into Aubrey Lake or extended from there down the Mississagi River to Lake Huron. (See Route 69.) Fishing: pike.

Detailed information *Mississagi River Canoe Route (Aubrey Falls to Lake Huron)*

Source Ministry of Natural Resources, Box 190, 62 Queen Street, Blind River, Ontario P0R 1B0

Detailed information *Wenebegon Canoe Route*

Source Ministry of Natural Resources, 34 Birch Street, Chapleau, Ontario P0M 1K0
or
Ministry of Natural Resources, Box 190, 62 Queen Street, Blind River, Ontario P0R 1B0

Route (71) Aubinadong River

Type River route

Rating B A B B

Length 98 km / 5 days

Portages 16

Main bodies of water Five Mile and Kingdon Lakes, Aubinadong River

Start Five Mile Lake by road (Hwy 129)

Finish Mississagi River by road (Hwy 129)

Intermediate access Honey Lake Road at the halfway point and Ranger Lake Road near the end

Beginning in Five Mile Lake Provincial Park, this route is dominated by high rock faces along the Aubinadong River and an abundance of white pine along the entire corridor. Partially burned over in the great 1948 Mississagi fire, the area has long felt the imprint of the logging industry, and old logging camps, roads, bridges and log jams are still evident. Moose are common; osprey may be sighted on Five Mile Lake; and lynx roam through the burnt-over area. River travel varies from wide, slow-moving stretches to narrow channels of fast water.

At most times of the year the water level is very low, and the route is normally passable only in May and June. When water levels are high, sections of fast water can be run by experienced canoeists. The route can be extended downstream on the Mississagi River to Lake Huron. (See Route 69.) Fishing: northern pike; brook trout in feeder streams.

Route (72) Ranger Lake Loop

Type Lake and river route

Rating B B B B

Length 110 km / 9 to 10 days

Portages 16 / 1 km

Main bodies of water Ranger, Saymo and Gong Lakes, West Aubinadong River, Megisan and Prairie Grass Lakes, Nushatogaini River

Start / Finish Ranger Lake by road (Hwy 556)

Opened up in the 1800s to log the hardwood stands, the Ranger Lake area is now forested with birch, sugar maple, white and jack pine and white spruce. These lakes and rivers offer a wilderness trip with opportunities to view fur-bearing mammals, such as beaver, mink, otter, fox and wolf. Some black bear and moose also live in the area. A few cottages and a tourist camp are scattered along Ranger and Saymo Lakes.

This route is not greatly affected by low water levels in summer. Fishing: lake trout, brook trout.

Detailed information *Aubinadong Canoe Route*

Source Ministry of Natural Resources,
34 Birch Street, Chapleau, Ontario P0M 1K0

Detailed information *Aubinadong River Canoe Route (East Branch)*. This brochure describes the second half of the route.

Source Ministry of Natural Resources,
Box 190, 62 Queen Street, Blind River, Ontario P0R 1B0

Detailed information *Ranger Lake Circle Route*

Source Ministry of Natural Resources,
Box 130, 69 Church Street, Sault Ste. Marie, Ontario P6A 5L5

Route (73) Goulais River

Type River route

Rating B C B B

Length 64 km / 5 to 6 days

Portages 25

Main bodies of water Ragged and Tepee Lakes, Goulais River

Start Ragged Lake by road (Hwy 556)

Finish Searchmont by road (off Hwy 556)

This route travels through the hardwood forest that borders the north shore of Lake Superior. The initial sixteen kilometres flow through an area devastated by forest fire in the mid 1960s. Logging first attracted settlement in the early 1800s, when men arrived to cut timber for the large mill at Searchmont. Today, the village of Searchmont is the only settlement along this route. If time permits, side trips can be made into connecting lakes.

Some portages are not easily seen, and four portages are required to bypass dangerous falls. Fishing: pike, pickerel.

Route (74) Batchawana River

Type River route

Rating A n/a B B

Length 49 km / 3 to 4 days

Portages 9 / 2.2 km

Main bodies of water Batchawana River

Start Batchawana Station by rail (Algoma Central)

Finish Hwy 17 just above Batchawana Bay

Flowing into Lake Superior, the Batchawana River traverses scenic Algoma interior country. Originally home to the Ojibway nation, this area became a rich source of furs for the Hudson's Bay Company in the 1800s. Birch, sugar maple, aspen, pine and spruce can be found along the river, and sandbars provide good campsites. There are no buildings on this wilderness route, but the river does touch old logging roads at points.

May and June are the best months for this trip, but the water will be extremely cold. Low water levels later in the summer require considerable wading and additional portaging. Fishing: brook trout, rainbow trout.

Detailed information *Goulais River Canoe Route*

Source Ministry of Natural Resources,
Box 130, 69 Church Street, Sault Ste. Marie, Ontario P6A 5L5

Detailed information *Batchawana River Canoe Route*

Source Ministry of Natural Resources,
Box 130, 69 Church Street, Sault Ste. Marie, Ontario P6A 5L5

Route (75) The Coastal Trip

Type Lake route

Rating n/a A n/a A

Length 160 km / 10 days

Portages 0

Main body of water Lake Superior

Start Marathon by road (Hwy 17)

Finish Michipicoten Harbour by road (Hwy 17)

Following the beautiful and rugged shore of Lake Superior, this route offers a unique experience for the accomplished, weather-wise canoeist. A harsh, two-day run for the voyageurs' fur-laden *canots de maître*, today this trip is more often taken at a leisurely pace. Indeed, the pace may be even more leisurely than expected, for heavy winds can keep the canoeist in camp for days at a time. The semi-mountainous wilderness of Pukaskwa National Park descends to the Lake Superior shore in a jagged, labyrinthine fortress of rock formations. Prehistoric man used boulders to build pits and cairns on the beaches. Archaeologists call these the Pukaskwa Pits, and there is debate as to whether they were used as places of worship or for storing catches of fish. Recent human artifacts include the occasional trapper's cabin and the abandoned remains of fishing and logging camps. Only on Otter Island is there human settlement — a lodge, lighthouse and commercial fishery — and these stand empty for part of each year. Excellent campsites shelter in small bays and inlets, and driftwood provides abundant firewood. Side trips can be made up the numerous rivers flowing into Lake Superior.

This trip requires extreme caution at all times and is recommended only for experienced canoeists. Weather conditions change quickly, and suitable landing spots on the exposed rock shore are often difficult to find. Sudden fogs and drizzle can give the canoeist as much trouble as the wind and waves: He or she can expect to be shore-bound one day in every three. Summer water temperature averages 4°C; a scantily clad person will survive only thirty minutes. Floater coats are recommended. Fishing: lake trout, rainbow trout, whitefish, pike; brook trout in rivers.

Detailed information *The Coastal Trip*

Source Pukaskwa National Park,
Box 550, Marathon, Ontario P0T 2E0

Area (M) White River

Type Lake and river routes

Length 6 documented routes / 20 to 192 km / 1 to 8 days

Main bodies of water Obatanga, Knife and Hammer Lakes, Depew River, White Lake, Kwinkwaga, White and Bremner Rivers, Lake Superior

Access Various points by road off Hwys 17 and 631

These 5575 square kilometres of wilderness canoe country abut Lake Superior and extend inland, with the town of White River and Hwy 17 roughly in the centre of the area. High, exposed granite outcrops alternate with pockets of sandy soil, where boreal species, such as black spruce and jack pine, grow. The area offers a good variety of canoeing conditions. The precipitous dropping away of the Canadian Shield towards Lake Superior has resulted in many rapids, most of which can be portaged. Slow, meandering sections of river give way to chutes, rapids, gorges and waterfalls, such as the thirty-metre Umbata

Falls on the White River. In addition to exciting river travel, this area also includes large, deep lakes; tiny, wind-protected lakes and marshes.

Because of abundant beaver dams and rapid drops in elevation in the area, portages are frequent on most routes. However, very few are unusually long. Travel on Lake Superior is for experienced canoeists only. The waves, winds and cold water of Lake Superior pose constant hazards. Fishing: pickerel, pike, whitefish, brook trout, rainbow trout, sturgeon, salmon.

Detailed information

White River Canoe Route
(Hwy 17 to Lake Superior, ending at Heron Bay)
192 km / 8 to 10 days / 58 portages (The longest is 2.2 km.)
Mainly a river route, with an eight-kilometre section on Lake Superior, the White River offers a possible side trip to White Lake and the impressive Umbata Falls. The Pukaskwa Pits, ancient rock cairns and pits, can be found on the Lake Superior shore.

Canoeing White Lake
(White Lake and surrounding small lakes and rivers)
10 to 40 km / 1 to 2 days / 8 portages
Ideal for leisurely paddling and fishing, White Lake and its tributary lakes and rivers offer at least three possible short trips into scenic country of historic interest. White Lake is large enough to be dangerous in windy weather.

The Bremner River Canoe Route (Pinei or McCrea Lake to Hwy 17)
71 km / 4 days / 25 portages
Canoeists can either fly in to isolated Pinei or McCrea Lake or paddle from Hwy 17 up the Bremner River to these lakes and return the same way, in which case the figures given above must be doubled. The Bremner River is wide and slow-moving for most of its length.

The Kwinkwaga River Canoe Route
(Kakakiwibik Lake on Hwy 631 to White Lake on Hwy 17)
110 km / 6 days / 27 portages
This route consists of a chain of small lakes connected by the Kwinkwaga River. Of special interest is a large marshy area where moose, waterfowl and other wildlife may be observed.

The Depew River Canoe Route (Hwy 17 or 631 to the White River)
50 km / 3 to 4 days / 38 portages
The picturesque Depew River links a chain of small lakes that flow south and then west into the White River. This is a relatively easy route. The figures given above represent the maximum trip possible; several shorter versions can also be canoed.

Obatanga Provincial Park Canoe Route
(Numerous starting and finishing points off Hwy 17)
100 km / 5 to 7 days / 8 portages
Many variations in length and direction are possible on this route, which consists of small, river-linked lakes.

Source Ministry of Natural Resources,
Box 1160, 22 Mission Road, Wawa, Ontario P0S 1K0

Area (N) Lake Superior Provincial Park

Type Lake and river routes

Length 4 documented routes / 13 to 110 km / 2 to 9 days

Main bodies of water Sand Lake, Sand River, Mijinemungshing and Old Woman Lakes, Anjigami River, Anjigami Lake, Michipicoten River, Belanger Lake, Lake Superior

Access By road, Hwys 17 and 101; by rail, Algoma Central Railway

These routes follow waterways once used by the Ojibway, who hunted inland in winter and in spring camped at the river mouths on Lake Superior to fish and make maple sugar. The high, dramatic cliffs along Lake Superior furnished them with many places sacred to their religion and myths, including the famous Agawa Rock, with its faded pictographs. In later times rivers like the Anjigami were used by loggers, and remnants of their old dams and sluices can still be found. This is rugged country, with maple-capped hills predominating. These hills fall away to steep cliffs on one side and more gradual, water-worked slopes on the other, covered with mixed coniferous and deciduous trees. The valley bottoms, with their finer, wetter soils, have given rise to black spruce forests. The rivers are often boulder-strewn, with rapids and scenic waterfalls marking their descent toward Lake Superior.

Three of these routes can be combined to make loop trips. The larger lakes can be dangerous on windy days, and the waves, winds and cold water of Lake Superior are extremely hazardous. The Sand River route can be dangerous during the spring runoff. August water levels throughout the area may require more portaging and wading. Fishing: brook trout, lake trout, pickerel, pike; rainbow trout, coho and pink salmon, lake sturgeon in the Michipicoten River.

Detailed information *Canoeing in Lake Superior Provincial Park*

Source Ministry of Natural Resources,
Box 1160, 22 Mission Road, Wawa, Ontario P0S 1K0

Area (O) Sudbury

Type River and lake routes

Length 9 documented routes / 48 to 200 km / 4 to 10 days

Main bodies of water Spanish, Onaping, Vermilion, Wanapitei, Sturgeon Rivers and Lakes

Access Various points by road off Hwys 17, 144, 541 and 560

This area is characterized by bedrock hills and ridges with shallow, drift-filled valleys. Numerous lakes of various sizes and meandering streams combine with five major river systems flowing southward through pine forests. Originally inhabited by the Ojibway, the region was exploited during the fur trade era, and Hudson's Bay Company posts stood on Wanapitei and Whitefish Lakes. Logging took place at the turn of the century, and much of the area is still under logging license. The discovery of nickel in 1883 led to the development of the mining industry that is the mainstay of Sudbury today. Hydro-electric dams are located on the Spanish, Vermilion and Wanapitei Rivers. Most of the area is in a wild, natural state, with settlement concentrated around Sudbury. The valley north of Sudbury includes agricultural and residential development.

Most of the routes in this area are best canoed in spring and early summer. Portages are usually frequent and short. The eastern routes connect with the Temagami Canoe Area (P). Drinking water should be treated. Fishing: pickerel, pike, smallmouth bass, perch, brook trout, lake trout.

Detailed information *Sudbury Area Canoe Routes* (Map). Descriptions of specific routes can be found in the following brochures.

Route A Sturgeon River (McCullough Lake to Wanapitei Lake)
112 km / 8 to 10 days / 25 portages

Route B Sturgeon River (McCullough Lake to Glen Afton)
112 km / 8 to 10 days / 31 portages
The Sturgeon River offers two rugged wilderness routes, featuring considerable white water for experienced canoeists.

Route C North Wanapitei River
200 km / 8 to 10 days / 31 portages
Beginning in the north end of the canoe area, this route offers challenging stretches of white water.

Route D Wanapitei Lake and Vicinity
72 km / 5 to 7 days / 11 portages
This route offers scenic, interconnected lake travel. Caution is required on large bodies of water.

Route E South Wanapitei River (Wanapitei Lake to Georgian Bay)
200 km / 8 to 10 days / 16 portages
There is some white water along this route, which ends on Georgian Bay.

Route F Onaping River
48 km / 4 to 6 days
Although there is some lake travel at the beginning, this is predominantly a river route, with many rapids in the final stages.

Route 19 (Part One) Vermilion River (Thor Lake to Capreol)
69 km / 5 to 7 days / 36 portages

Route 19 (Part Two) Vermilion River (Bass Lake to McCharles Lake)
72 km / 5 to 7 days / 13 portages
The Vermilion River routes offer slow, steady trips, thanks to shallow waters and extensive meanders.

Route 21 Spanish River
200 km / 8 to 10 days
There are some stretches of white water along this river route.
(See Route 62 in this book.)

Source Ministry of Natural Resources, Box 3500, Postal Station A, Sudbury, Ontario P3A 4S2

Area (P) Temagami

Type Lake and river routes

Length 22 documented routes / 13 to 208 km / 1 to 14 days

Main bodies of water Lake Temagami, Temagami River, Wanapitei Lake, Sturgeon River, Lady Evelyn Lake, Red Cedar Lake, Montreal River

Access Numerous points by road on Lake Temagami and in the surrounding area

Temagami's 10 000 square kilometres of canoe country offer a wide variety of river and lake routes lying in the watersheds of the Montreal, Sturgeon and Ottawa Rivers. One of the largest lakes in the region is Lake Temagami, whose name in the Ojibway language means "deep water by the shore". Its deep, clear waters, abundance of islands and extremely irregular shape typify the lakes of the region. These waterways are particularly attractive to the canoeist because they readily lend themselves to loop or circle routes.

The Temagami Indian band of Bear Island have hunted, fished and trapped in the area for centuries. Because the main trade and travel routes of the Indians and French lay 100 kilometres to the south along the Mattawa and French Rivers, white settlement did not come into the area until 1850, when the Hudson's Bay Company built a post on Temagami Island. It was later moved to Bear Island, where the building still stands.

The railroad pushed through this area in 1902 to link farmers in New Liskeard with the markets of southern Ontario. It eventually brought mining and logging to the region. Temagami's vast stands of virgin pine did not fall to the axe until the 1920s. Today, remains of old logging camps are still visible along some of the canoe routes. Mining in the area began in the early 1900s with discoveries of nickel, cobalt and silver at Cobalt. Iron was discovered near the town of Temagami in 1897. The Sherman Mine, which produces large quantities of iron ore, operates just north of the town.

The forest of the region is a transitional mix of northern evergreens and various hardwoods. On well-drained sites the common species is pine; white and red pine thrive on rocky shores and ridges, jack pine on burnt-over areas. Some of the white pines on Lake Temagami date back 300 years. They have survived thanks to an extensive shoreline timber reserve that has limited lumbering and cottage construction. A wide selection of wetland communities thrive in this region; they include marshes, floating bogs and black spruce bogs. Temagami country is a rolling plain of rock-knob uplands covered with shallow, sandy soil. Many sandy beaches can be found on the larger lakes, and rugged cliffs are common in the bedrock areas. Its great natural beauty has made the area a favourite for holidayers, and though summer camps, cottages and resorts are fairly common, most of the shoreline remains undeveloped. Most portages are rocky but well cleared. Fishing: pike, pickerel, lake trout.

Detailed information *Temagami Canoe Routes* ($2.00). This excellent booklet contains maps and descriptions of twenty-two possible routes as well as information on the area and camping techniques.

Source Ministry of Natural Resources, Box 38, Temagami, Ontario P0H 2H0

Route

76 Mattawa River
77 French River
78 Restoule-Upper French River Loop
79 Dokis Loop
80 Mercer Lake-Little French River Loop
81 Wolf and Pickerel Rivers
82 Pickerel River Loop
83 Magnetawan River Loop
84 South Georgian Bay Loop
85 Gibson-McDonald Loop
86 South Branch Muskoka River
87 Poker Lake Loop
88 Black Lake Loop
89 Wildcat Lake Loop

90 Burnt River
91 Indian River
92 Skootamatta River
93 Moira River
94 Kishkebus Loop
95 Mississippi River-Big Gull Lake Loop
96 Mississippi River
97 Charleston Lake-Gananoque Lake Loop
98 Nottawasaga River
99 Beaver River
100 Rankin River
101 Saugeen River
102 Maitland River
(Continued opposite)

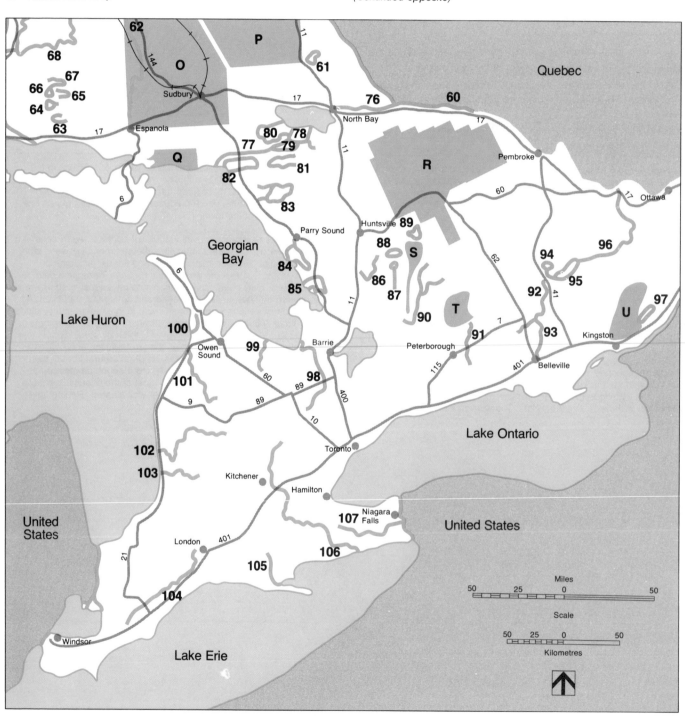

103 Bayfield River
104 Lower Thames River
105 Big Creek
106 Grand River
107 Welland River

Area

Q Killarney Provincial Park
R Algonquin Provincial Park
S Gull River
T North Kawartha
U Cataraqui

Route (76) Mattawa River

Type River and lake route

Rating C B B C

Length 64 km / 2 to 3 days

Portages 11

Main bodies of water Trout Lake, Lake Talon, Mattawa River

Start Trout Lake by road (Hwy 63)

Finish Mattawa by road (Hwy 17)

Intermediate access Samuel de Champlain Provincial Park by road (Hwy 17)

One of the most historically significant waterways in Canada, the Mattawa River, a tributary of the Ottawa River, was used originally by the Indians as a route to Lake Nipissing and Georgian Bay. Etienne Brulé and Samuel de Champlain were among the first Europeans to travel the Mattawa River in the early 1600s, and they were soon followed by missionaries and a steady stream of voyageurs. A crucial link in the rich fur trade, the course of the Mattawa River was described over the next two centuries in the diaries of explorers and traders from the North West Company and the Hudson's Bay Company. In the 1880s lumber operations reached the large stands of Mattawa white pine, and ruins of an old logging camp are still evident near Paresseux Falls. The Mattawa River is also rich in scenery and wildlife. Running in an ancient geological fault, the river flows over waterfalls and past black granite cliffs and veins of mica. Talon Chutes and Paresseux Falls are the two most spectacular waterfalls. Upriver from Paresseux Falls *Portage de la cave* skirts an area of obstacles on the river and takes the canoeist through a gloomy ravine. Below *Portage Paresseux* the riverbanks rise into cliffs and to the left is a large, shallow cave, which was called *La Porte de l'enfer* ("the gates of hell") by the voyageurs. A few rapids and riffles mark the Mattawa River before it enters Samuel de Champlain Provincial Park, where an exhibition, which includes an authentic reproduction of a *canot de maître*, tells more of the history of the river and the fur trade era. The trip can end here or be extended sixteen kilometres to the historic village of Mattawa, which grew around an early Hudson's Bay Company post.

Most of this route is located within Mattawa River Provincial Park, and campsites are adequate. A number of private cottages dot the shores of Trout Lake and Lake Talon. Windy weather can make both these lakes hazardous. Drinking water should be treated. This route can be extended from Mattawa down the Ottawa River. (See Route 60.) Fishing: pike, pickerel, bass, lake trout.

Route (77) French River

Type River route

Rating B B C B

Length 77 km / 5 to 7 days

Portages 7

Main bodies of water French River

Start Chaudiere Dam by road (off Hwy 64)

Finish French River Village by road (Hwy 607)

Intermediate access Dokis Bay by road (Dokis Indian Reserve Road), Hwy 69

The French River is rich in history and has served as part of a major trade route between the Ottawa River and Georgian Bay since prehistoric times. European explorers, missionaries and fur traders came to the river in the early 1600s, and both Samuel de Champlain and Alexander Mackenzie wrote vivid descriptions of this waterway. After the fur trade began to decline in the nineteenth century, timber operations moved into the area, and with them the first settlers. A thriving sawmill community, French River Village, grew up at the river's main outlet into Georgian Bay, and ruins of the village can still be seen. The French River is now used almost exclusively as a recreational resource. Resembling a series of connecting lakes descending in stages toward the Bay, the French River challenges experienced canoeists with numerous rapids, chutes and falls. Along its length the river shoreline offers a varied landscape of heavy pine forest, bare rock, hills and small secluded beaches. A number of cottages and hunt camps are found along the way. Legends and folklore cling to several spots on the river, including Owl's Head and Lost Child Bend. A stone cross on a hill below Crooked Rapids is said to mark the spot where early missionaries were martyred at the stake. Beyond Recollet Falls, another spot associated with missionary legends, only two sets of rapids separate the canoeist from Georgian Bay. At Ox Bay the canoeist can choose to return to Hwy 69 or Lake Nipissing via the French or Pickerel River rather than descending into Georgian Bay.

Georgian Bay requires extra caution in windy weather. Drinking water should be treated. Fishing: northern pike, pickerel, smallmouth bass, muskellunge.

Detailed information *Mattawa River Provincial Park*

Source Ministry of Natural Resources, Box 3070, 222 McIntyre Street West, North Bay, Ontario P1B 8K7

Detailed information *French River Canoe Route*

Source Ministry of Natural Resources, Box 3070, 222 McIntyre Street West, North Bay, Ontario P1B 8K7

Route (78) Restoule-Upper French River Loop

Type Lake and river route

Rating C A B B

Length 72 km / 4 to 6 days

Portages 14

Main bodies of water Patterson and Restoule Lakes, Restoule and French Rivers

Start / Finish Restoule Provincial Park by road (off Hwy 534)

Intermediate access Patterson Lake by road (Restoule Provincial Park Road)

At the beginning of this trip the Restoule River flows into scenic Lennon Lake, where red and white pine, poplar and white birch cover the rocky shore. Beyond Lennon Lake the Restoule River widens and meanders through a marshy area good for wildlife viewing. A scenic gorge and falls are impressive sights on Restoule Bay, which opens into the French River. The shoreline changes markedly along the French River, with large stretches of open, flat rock and jack pine. The canoeist paddles up the French into the Upper French River, where there is no current because the Upper French is actually part of Lake Nipissing. Numerous pine-covered, rocky islands dot the large open stretches of the Upper French, and fishing and campsites are excellent. The canoeist then follows Shoal Creek and two small lakes towards Restoule Provincial Park. Shoal Creek winds through a flat, marshy area flooded by beaver dams, and wildlife is particularly abundant along this eight-kilometre section of the trip. Bass Lake is a good place to fish for bass, pickerel and pike. The portage trail out of Bass Lake is marked by impressive stands of red and white pine.

Poison ivy flourishes at points along this route. The larger lakes can be hazardous in windy weather. Fishing: pike, pickerel, largemouth bass, smallmouth bass, muskellunge.

Route (79) Dokis Loop

Type River and lake route

Rating C B B B

Length 90 km / 5 to 6 days

Portages 22 / 1.2 km, 1 km

Main bodies of water Patterson Lake, Restoule River, Memesagamesing Lake, Memesagamesing and French Rivers

Start / Finish Restoule Provincial Park by road (off Hwy 534)

Intermediate access Memesagamesing Lake by road (off Hwy 522)

A variation of Route 78, this trip follows waters that were used to transport logs to the French River in the late 1800s. After entering the widest section of scenic Lennon Lake, the canoeist must portage to Memesagamesing Lake. Numerous islands and bays dot this lake and can make navigation confusing. The entire north shore is part of the Dokis Indian Reserve, and several tourist camps are located on the lake. The Memesagamesing River, which follows, will require most of one day to travel; beaver dams, rapids and portages impede progress on this sixteen-kilometre stretch. Ruins of two old logging dams and one large log jam are also evident along this section. Continuing up the wide, lake-like French River, the canoeist will pass through a maze of islands with rocky, pine-dotted shores. On the return stretch of the Restoule River there are marshy areas where wildlife abounds.

Poison ivy flourishes at points along this route. Windy weather can make the lakes hazardous. Fishing: pike, pickerel, largemouth bass, smallmouth bass, muskellunge.

Detailed information *Restoule-Upper French Canoe Route*

Source Ministry of Natural Resources,
Box 3070, 222 McIntyre Street West, North Bay, Ontario P1B 8K7

Detailed information *Dokis Canoe Route*

Source Ministry of Natural Resources,
Box 3070, 222 McIntyre Street West, North Bay, Ontario P1B 8K7

Route (80) Mercer Lake-Little French River Loop

Type Lake and river route

Rating C A B B

Length 140 km / 7 to 10 days

Portages 6 / 1 km

Main bodies of water Mercer Lake, Little French and Wolseley Rivers, Lake Nipissing, Upper French River

Start / Finish Mercer Lake by road (off Hwy 64)

Intermediate access Little French River by road (Dokis Indian Reserve Road), Wolseley Bay by road (Hwy 528), Wolseley River by road (Hwy 64), Sucker Creek Landing by road (Hwy 64)

A circuit that includes part of the historic French River voyageur route, this trip travels for approximately half of its distance on vast Lake Nipissing. Beginning on Mercer Lake, where steep, rocky banks alternate with low, marshy sections, the route then proceeds down the Hall River. This stretch is distinguished by a wetland habitat that is excellent for wildlife viewing. The canoeist then follows the Little French River through a region bordered by large white pine. This landscape changes to low shores and jack pine on the approach to Five Finger Rapids, scenic but extremely dangerous rapids that must be portaged over bald rock to the French River. The island-dotted French River flows past Wolseley Bay, where supplies, telephone and road access are available. From here a series of small lakes lead to Deer Bay of Lake Nipissing. The second half of the trip follows West Bay and the southwest shore of Lake Nipissing, turning into the French River and returning up the Hall River to Mercer Lake. Six side trips are also possible, some at marked portages and some with no portages necessary.

Canoes must be lined upstream and carried over beaver dams in several places along the French River. Extreme caution is required on Lake Nipissing, where the shallow waters can become rough very quickly. Early morning, when the water is calm, is the best time to paddle this stretch. Campsites are available along the French River, but since much of the land along the Wolseley River is private property, camping is discouraged on this stretch. The one long portage must be made by compass through dense bush into Deer Bay; there is no trail. Drinking water should be treated. Poison ivy flourishes at points along this route. Fishing: pike, pickerel, bass.

Route (81) Wolf and Pickerel Rivers

Type River and lake route

Rating B B C C

Length 51 km / 3 days

Portages 2

Main bodies of water Wolf River, Dollars and Kawigamog Lakes, Pickerel River, Wauquimakog Lake

Start Wolf River by road (off Hwy 522 at Loring)

Finish Port Loring by road (Hwy 522)

Intermediate access Ess Narrows by road (Hwy 522)

Pine and mixed hardwood forest covers the granite and gneiss shoreline of the Wolf and Pickerel Rivers. Most of the shore is Crown land, except where cottages are found, primarily in the vicinity of Dollars and Kawigamog Lakes and Port Loring. From about 1912 the steamboat *Kawigamog* worked Dollars Lake, towing log booms and carrying goods. Pine Lake Dam, near the beginning of the trip, is a scenic high point during spring runoff.

Most of the seventeen campsites are in the Dollars Lake area, due to limited access along the rest of the shoreline. In Port Loring canoes can be rented and arrangements can be made for transportation back to the starting point. Fishing: pickerel, northern pike, largemouth bass, smallmouth bass.

Detailed information *Mercer Lake-Little French River Loop*

Source Ministry of Natural Resources,
Box 3070, 222 McIntyre Street West, North Bay, Ontario P1B 8K7

Detailed information *Pickerel and Wolf River Canoe Routes*

Source Ministry of Natural Resources,
4 Miller Street, Parry Sound, Ontario P2A 1S8

Route (82) Pickerel River Loop

Type River and lake route

Rating B B B C

Length 62 km / 4 days

Portages 11

Main bodies of water Gurd and Pakeshkag Lakes, Pickerel River, Key Inlet

Start / Finish Grundy Lake Provincial Park by road (off Hwys 69 and 522)

Intermediate access Marinas at Pickerel River and Key Inlet on Hwy 69

Beginning and ending in Grundy Lake Provincial Park, this route stretches along the glacially scoured shores of the Pickerel River, where barren granite or a sparse cover of scrub pine and juniper makes up the landscape. Key Inlet, which flows between canyon-like walls of pink granite, served as the traditional voyageur bypass of the dangerous mouth of the Pickerel River on Georgian Bay. These granite walls are marked by potholes, formed by the powerful forces of melting ice and moving boulders. The potholes, which can be explored by climbers, often create reservoirs for small ecological communities of trees, spagnum moss and orchids. Wildlife in the area includes beaver, moose, deer, marten, fisher and wolf. Human settlement is limited to cottages along Key Inlet and on the Pickerel River. Beyond Grundy Lake Provincial Park a section of the route traverses the French River Indian Reserve.

The mouth of the Pickerel River and Key Inlet are exposed to the winds and waters of Georgian Bay, and canoeists must be especially cautious along this section. Northwesterly winds sometimes blow along the river, making canoeing impossible. Marsh conditions at the north end of Pakeshkag Lake dry up in the summer months, and this section may require a longer portage. Canoes can be rented in the vicinity of Grundy Lake Provincial Park. Fishing: pickerel, northern pike, muskellunge, smallmouth bass.

Route (83) Magnetawan River Loop

Type Lake and river route

Rating B B B B

Length 120 km / 4 to 7 days

Portages 18 / 2.3 km, 2.4 km, 1.4 km, 1.4 km

Main bodies of water Wahwashkesh Lake, North Magnetawan River, Harris Lake, South Magnetawan River, Big Bay, Miskokway and Bolger Lakes

Start / Finish Wahwashkesh Lake by road (off Hwy 520)

Intermediate access Harris and Naiscoot Lakes by road (off Hwy 69)

This circular route flows through a representative southern Shield landscape of predominantly pine and birch forest and gneiss and granite outcrops. The area is steeped in the history of the white pine logging era, and remnants of dams, camboose camps and loggers' graves can be explored at various points. The Magnetawan River created several obstacles for the lumbermen. It flowed away from the markets centred on the St. Lawrence; prevailing winds could stall log drives to the American Midwest for days; and the frequent rapids had to be navigated precisely to prevent massive log jams. At Carve Island wind-bound log drivers developed a tradition of carving logged pine stumps into birds and animals. The wildlife of the area includes beaver, bear, deer, moose, otter, mink, great blue heron, merganser, ruffed grouse and woodcock. Cottages line Wahwashkesh, Harris and Maple Lakes, and settlement is low to medium along the South Magnetawan River. On the North Magnetawan, however, human habitation is limited to an occasional hunt camp.

Canoeists will be exposed to moderately challenging white water and will need a general understanding of river travel. The route is passable throughout the canoeing season by canoeists with whitewater experience, except for the Crooked Rapids, which become a series of falls and ponds in the summer. Major rapids are potentially hazardous during spring runoff. Variations in this route make possible a shorter circular route or either of two linear trips. These are shown in the brochure. Campsites are abundant, but problems with latrine facilities (due to shallow soil cover) and difficulties docking canoes along the steep shoreline must be considered. Drinking water from lakes with dense cottage development requires treatment. Fishing: pickerel, pike, perch, smallmouth bass, lake trout; ciscoe in lakes.

Detailed information *Pickerel and Wolf River Canoe Routes*

Source Ministry of Natural Resources, 4 Miller Street, Parry Sound, Ontario P2A 1S8

Detailed information *Magnetawan River Canoe Route*

Source Ministry of Natural Resources, 4 Miller Street, Parry Sound, Ontario P2A 1S8

Route (84) South Georgian Bay Loop

Type Lake and river route

Rating B B B C

Length 150 km / 3 to 7 days

Portages 30 / 1.3 km

Main bodies of water Georgian Bay, Moon River, Otter, Three Legged, Crane, Blackstone and Healey Lakes

Start / Finish Parry Sound by road (Hwy 69B)

Intermediate access Healey Lake by road (off Hwy 612), Crane and Three Legged Lakes by road (off Hwy 69)

This route exposes the canoeist to a wide variety of scenery, ranging from the rugged 30 000 Islands along the Georgian Bay shoreline to rivers and placid inland lakes. The islands form a classic Georgian Bay landscape of wind-bent pine and barren rock. The stately cottages in the area were built between 1900 and 1930, many by wealthy Americans. Steamers, such as the *Midland City*, carried vacationers during this period. The moderate to heavy cottage development on the inland lakes is of a much more recent vintage. This route was significant for the Ojibway, who shifted their camps each spring to where the Blackstone River flows into Little Blackstone Lake to catch and smoke the spawning pickerel. After white men began to log this area, many of the portages were used during winter lumbering operations. The Moon River was used by the lumber companies to float logs from Lake Muskoka to Georgian Bay. From the mouth of the Moon River the logs were driven to the sawmills at Parry Sound. Inland, the rivers flow through sugar maple and beech forests and several bogs and swamps.

This route can be broken into numerous short, interconnected trips, which are sketched out in the brochure listed below. The winds and waters of Georgian Bay occasionally create hazardous canoeing conditions. The only fast water is along the Moon River in the spring. This segment should be canoed with caution at all times, however, because the dam at Bala can cause the water level to fluctuate rapidly. Only six campsites are maintained in the area, due to limited soil cover. Drinking water should be carried for use on small lakes and along heavily populated stretches. Fishing: northern pike, rock bass, largemouth bass, smallmouth bass, lake trout, rainbow trout, yellow perch, walleye, muskellunge.

Detailed information *South Georgian Bay Canoe Routes*

Source Ministry of Natural Resources,
4 Miller Street, Parry Sound, Ontario P2A 1S8

Route (85) Gibson-McDonald Loop

Type Lake and river route

Rating B B C B

Length 56 km / 3 days

Portages 9

Main bodies of water Six Mile and Gibson Lakes, Gibson River, Georgian Bay, McCrae and McDonald Lakes

Start / Finish Six Mile Lake Provincial Park by road (Hwy 69)

Intermediate access Georgian Bay Road off Hwy 69

Winding between sloping granite shores with white pine, second-growth maple and stunted oaks, the Gibson-McDonald offers a pleasant trip for novices through some of the most rugged scenery in Muskoka. Near the junction of the Musquash and Gibson Rivers submerged logs and iron rungs are reminders of the old logging industry that once fed the sawmills in the town of Muskoka Mills. Of interest are the falls of Three Rock Chute and the shrine at the entrance to McCrae Lake. Canoeists will encounter cottages and boat traffic on Georgian Bay and Six Mile Lake.

Wind and water conditions on Georgian Bay occasionally create canoeing hazards. A slightly longer variation of this route extends the stretch along Georgian Bay and returns to Six Mile Lake Provincial Park via South Bay, Little Go Home Bay and Gloucester Pool. This extension is described in the second brochure listed below. Fishing: bass, pike, pickerel, muskellunge.

Detailed information *Canoeing the Gibson-McDonald*

Source Ministry of Natural Resources,
Midhurst, Ontario L0L 1X0

Detailed information *South Georgian Bay Canoe Routes*

Source Ministry of Natural Resources,
4 Miller Street, Parry Sound, Ontario P2A 1S8

Route (86) South Branch Muskoka River

Type River route

Rating C C C C

Length 42 km / 2 days

Portages 11

Main bodies of water Lake of Bays, South Muskoka River

Start Baysville by road (Hwy 117)

Finish Bracebridge by road (Hwy 11)

For centuries the Muskoka River was a major transportation artery for native tribes, but it was not until 1826, when Lt. Briscoe of the Royal Engineers travelled this route, that a white man crossed the heart of what is now known as Muskoka. The river flows south through rugged terrain characteristic of the Canadian Shield. In addition to numerous stretches of forested land and rock formations, several scenic waterfalls and rapids add to the natural beauty. Wildlife is normally limited to smaller mammals, such as beaver, otter and mink. Much of this route is surrounded by privately owned land, and cottages are scattered along the length of the river. Four dams are also located on this route.

Campsites are limited to two sections of Crown land on the upper portion of the trip and one commercial campsite approximately midway. Drinking water should be treated. The trip can be extended six kilometres to Muskoka Lake, but motorboats abound on this stretch of the river. Fishing: brook trout, bass.

Route (87) Poker Lake Loop

Type Lake route

Rating n/a C C C

Length 17 km / 1 to 2 days

Portages 9

Main bodies of water Cinder, Poker and Big East Lakes

Start / Finish Cinder Lake by road (Ministry of Natural Resources access road)

Intermediate access Big East Lake by road (County Road 1)

This route through a series of small lakes provides a safe, interesting canoe trip for the beginner. Lumbered and burnt over several times in the past two centuries, this area contains relics of two of the more recent logging operations, including an old timber dam at the outlet of Big East Lake, a sunken logging boat on the northwest shore of Cinder Lake and the ruins of an old logging camp on the eastern shore. Wildlife attractions include nesting osprey on an island in Poker Lake and an active heronry on one of the small, unnamed lakes. A typical Canadian Shield landscape surrounds these waterways, with a mixture of bare rock ridges, shallow soils supporting hemlock and white pine, and deeper soils supporting mixed hardwood stands. The entire area is in Crown ownership, and no cottage development detracts from the natural setting.

Campsites are plentiful. Drinking water should be treated. Fishing: smallmouth bass, largemouth bass, brook trout.

Detailed information *Canoe Muskoka-Haliburton*

Source Ministry of Natural Resources,
Box 1138, Bracebridge, Ontario P0B 1C0

Detailed information *The Poker Lake Canoe Route*

Source Ministry of Natural Resources,
Minden, Ontario K0M 2K0

Route (88) Black Lake Loop

Type Lake and river route

Rating C C B C

Length 22 km / 2 days

Portages 11 / 1.5 km

Main bodies of water Raven and Black Lakes, Black River

Start / Finish Raven Lake by road (off Hwy 35)

Intermediate access The route crosses Hwy 35 east of Wren Lake.

Since commercial development has been restricted in most of this area, the Black Lake route combines a short, accessible trip with virtually untouched wilderness. Cherished by local Indian tribes for its excellent hunting, this area is still home to numerous species of mammals and waterfowl. Once considered as a possible communications link between Lake Simcoe and Ottawa, the Black River meanders through marshland and churns over rapids and several waterfalls. Granites are the most common rocks throughout this representative section of the Canadian Shield. A few white pine are scattered through the maple-spruce forest, and a wide variety of aquatic plant life flourishes in the marshes. Some cottages have been built along the lakes adjacent to Hwy 35.

Although this is a good route for the novice, the Black River requires extra caution when canoeing in the fast and cold water of early spring and late fall. Fishing: brook trout, rainbow trout, bass.

Route (89) Wildcat Lake Loop

Type Lake route

Rating C B B B

Length 43 km / 3 to 4 days

Portages 18 / 1 km, 1 km, 2.8 km

Main bodies of water Kawagama and Havelock Lakes

Start / Finish Kawagama Lake at three possible access points by road (off Hwy 35)

Rich in scenic beauty and history, this route follows a chain of lakes and interconnecting streams. Except for cottages on Kawagama, Bear and Kimball Lakes, the area is mostly uninhabited. Used to transport logs in relatively recent times, this route also passes by relics of a much earlier logging era, including dams, cadge roads and eye bolts secured in solid rock. The portage between Mink and Rockaway Lakes offers a view of some of the largest white pine in the adjacent white pine reserve. A wide variety of aquatic vegetation and waterfowl is found in the Gibson Marsh. In addition to numerous species of smaller mammals, this trip may also provide an opportunity to view moose, bear or deer. High cliffs tower over Bear Lake, and ice is sometimes found at the base of the cliffs in May, June or even July.

During periods of extreme low water it may be necessary to line the canoe through shallow sections. Part of this route passes through privately controlled land, and a fee is charged to camp here. Fishing: brook trout, lake trout, rainbow trout, smallmouth bass.

Detailed information *Canoe Muskoka-Haliburton*

Source Ministry of Natural Resources,
Box 1138, Bracebridge, Ontario P0B 1C0

Detailed information *Canoe Muskoka-Haliburton*

Source Ministry of Natural Resources,
Box 1138, Bracebridge, Ontario P0B 1C0

Route (90) Burnt River "A"

Type Lake and river route

Rating B B B C

Length 94 km / 2 to 3 days

Portages 15

Main bodies of water Head, Grass and Kashagawigamog Lakes, Drag and Burnt Rivers

Start Haliburton by road (Hwy 121)

Finish Balsam Lake Provincial Park by road (Hwy 48)

Intermediate access Several points by road off Hwys 121 and 519

The Burnt River once served Indian tribes returning from northern hunting grounds in the Algonquin Park region. Scenic falls and rapids are scattered along the entire route, and the Burnt River also offers numerous oxbow ponds and other meandering characteristics of a much older river. Wildlife includes great blue herons, loons, fur-bearing mammals and deer. The forest is largely mixed hardwoods, with some areas of white pine, red pine, hemlock and cedar. Most of the lakes and portions of the rivers have summer cottages dotting the shorelines.

Much of the land bordering this route is privately owned, and permission must be requested before camping. Motorboats are common during the summer. Drinking water should be treated. Caution is required on the approach to waterfalls. An alternative opening section of this route (designated in the brochure as Burnt River "B") is possible from Gooderham on Hwy 503 down the Irondale River to the junction of the Burnt River, twenty-four kilometres below Devil's Gap Dam. Fishing: brook trout, rainbow trout, muskellunge, pickerel.

Route (91) Indian River

Type River route

Rating B C C C

Length 42 km / 2 days

Portages 6 (many more during the dry season)

Main body of water Indian River

Start Stony Lake by road (County Road 6)

Finish Rice Lake by road (County Road 34 at Serpent Mounds Provincial Park)

Intermediate access Several points by road, particularly Warsaw Caves Conservation Area (County Road 4)

The Indian River begins at Stony Lake on the Canadian Shield, where cottages are frequent, and descends into farming country on the Great Lakes-St. Lawrence Lowlands. At the Warsaw Caves Conservation Area the river disappears underground to emerge 450 metres farther on between sixty-metre cliffs. Farther downstream the restored Hope Sawmill, Lang Gristmill and Lang Century Village are worth visiting. In its final stages the river meanders among the tear-shaped hills of the Peterborough Drumlin Field. From the wildfowl marsh at the mouth, a 400-metre paddle west brings you to Serpent Mounds Provincial Park.

Drinking water should be treated. The river runs through private property, but campsites can be found at two Conservation Areas and Serpent Mounds Provincial Park. This route is not recommended for travel after early July. Fishing: rock bass, smallmouth bass, largemouth bass, pickerel, muskellunge.

Detailed information *Canoe Routes on the Burnt River System*

Source Ministry of Natural Resources, Minden, Ontario K0M 2K0

Detailed information *The Indian River Canoe Route*

Source Otonabee Region Conservation Authority, 727 Lansdowne Street West, Peterborough, Ontario K9J 1Z2

Route (92) Skootamatta River

Type River route

Rating B B C C

Length 55 km / 1 to 2 days

Portages 15 to 20

Main bodies of water Skootamatta Lake, Skootamatta River

Start Skootamatta Lake by road (off Hwy 41)

Finish Tweed by road (Hwy 37)

Intermediate access Flinton by road (off Hwy 41)

Fast water and rapids are major features of this route. The northern Skootamatta River flows through relatively isolated, forested sections, but cottages and small towns increase in number as the river flows south. A portage at the nine-kilometre point marks the beginning of a shallow stretch of river bordered by swampy lands and congested with logs and beaver dams. A side trip can be taken near this point up Partridge Creek to Deerock Lake. Several old mills and remnants of the logging industry are landmarks on the trip. High Falls is particularly scenic.

Because of shallow water later in the season, this route should be canoed in spring or early summer. Drinking water should be treated. Fishing: pickerel, pike, bass, muskellunge, lake trout.

Route (93) Moira River

Type River route

Rating B B C C

Length 75 km / 2 to 3 days

Portages 13

Main bodies of water Moira River, Moira and Stoco Lakes

Start Brownson's Rapids by road (off Hwy 7)

Finish Cannifton by road (off Hwy 14)

Intermediate access Numerous points by road off Hwys 7 and 37

Few rapids mark the more isolated sections of the Moira River on its approach to the mouth of the Skootamatta River; but as the river turns south, swifts and white water become frequent. Five kilometres below the Skootamatta, ruins of a gristmill and dam announce the approach to Tweed, where Hwy 37 runs parallel to the Moira River. A one-day, eighteen-kilometre side trip up the Clare River can be added to the main route by crossing Stoco Lake at Tweed. Vanderwater Park, Plainfield Conservation Area and Thurlow Wildlife Area also border the southern reaches of the Moira. At Scuttles Holes, between Chisholm and Latta, legend has it that Indians fled into the caves with a booty of gold, but neither men nor treasure was ever seen again.

Some of the rapids offer challenging canoeing, but should be attempted by experienced paddlers only. Low water may cause some difficulties after mid June. During the high-water season the five kilometres from Cannifton to the Bay of Quinte are solid rapids, with large standing waves and numerous ledges that provide excellent canoeing and kayaking for whitewater experts. Drinking water should be treated. Fishing: pickerel, pike, bass, muskellunge.

Detailed information *Moira Watershed Canoe Routes*

Source Moira River Conservation Authority, 217 North Front Street, Belleville, Ontario K8P 3C3

Detailed information *Moira Watershed Canoe Routes*

Source Moira River Conservation Authority, 217 North Front Street, Belleville, Ontario K8P 3C3

Route (94) Kishkebus Loop

Type Lake route

Rating C B B C

Length 21 km / 1 day

Portages 4 / 1.5 km (rough terrain)

Main bodies of water Mazinaw, Kishkebus and Shabomeka Lakes

Start / Finish Bon Echo Provincial Park by road (Hwy 41)

This short route is travelled most frequently by campers based at Bon Echo Provincial Park. It traces the shorelines of large and small lakes and circles the spectacular Bon Echo Rock, with its pink granite and gneiss rock face towering 100 metres above Mazinaw Lake. The Indian pictographs on Bon Echo Rock are the most extensive collection of rock paintings in Ontario. There are occasional sightings of black bear and white-tailed deer in the area, and ospreys have been seen on Semicircle Lake. A memorial to the American poet, Walt Whitman (part of the Denison cultural legacy) is also located on this route. Cottages dot Mazinaw and Shabomeka Lakes; the rest of the route travels through an undeveloped landscape.

It is advisable to start this trip early in the day to take advantage of the morning calm on Upper Mazinaw Lake. Camping is not permitted in the Kishkebus area, and so there are no campsites maintained on this route. Drinking water should be treated. Fishing: lake trout, pickerel, bass, pike.

Detailed information *Kishkebus Canoe Route*

Source Ministry of Natural Resources, Metcalfe Street, Tweed, Ontario K0K 3J0

Route (95) Mississippi River-Big Gull Lake Loop

Type Lake and river route

Rating C B B C

Length 104 km / 5 days

Portages 13 / 1.4 km

Main bodies of water Mississippi River, Mazinaw, Kashwakamak and Big Gull Lakes

Start / Finish Bon Echo Provincial Park by road (Hwy 41)

Intermediate access Myers Cave by road (Hwy 506), Ardoch by road (off Hwy 506), Coxvale by road (between Hwys 506 and 509)

Nine lakes and the Mississippi River offer a variety of canoeing conditions along a route that combines an aura of remoteness with proximity to cottages, commercial campgrounds, township roads and camp stores. The Indians who first inhabited this area left few traces other than the extensive pictographs on the cliff face of Mazinaw Rock at Bon Echo Provincial Park. During the last century the Mississippi River was used to transport the great pines of the Mazinaw area to mills in Quebec. Of interest along the way are marble outcrops above Marble Lake and unusual aquatic vegetation in Mud Lake. The mixed deciduous forest is home to bears, deer, wolves, ospreys and turkey vultures.

Spring water conditions require additional caution and canoeing experience. Drinking water should be treated. An eight-day trip to the Ottawa River leaves this route at Crotch Lake. (See Route 96.) Fishing: pike, pickerel, bass, lake trout, brook trout.

Detailed information *Mississippi River-Big Gull Lake Canoe Route*

Source Ministry of Natural Resources, Metcalfe Street, Tweed, Ontario K0K 3J0

Detailed information *Pine Trees and Portages: A Mississippi Canoeing Experience*

Source Mississippi Valley Conservation Authority, Box 419, Carleton Place, Ontario K7C 3P5

Route (96) Mississippi River

Type Lake and river route

Rating B B B C

Length 200 km / 8 to 10 days

Portages 34 / 1 km

Main bodies of water Mazinaw, Kashwakamak, Crotch, Dalhousie and Mississippi Lakes, Mississippi River

Start Bon Echo Provincial Park by road (Hwy 41)

Finish Galetta by road (off Hwy 17)

Intermediate access Numerous points on township and county roads

The opening stretch of this route follows part of Route 95. At Crotch Lake the long trip down the Mississippi River begins, threading through picturesque towns, villages and farms as well as some remote stretches. Rapids and fast water are common. Used for transportation by Indians and loggers, the Mississippi River also powered saw and woollen mills during the late 1800s. Ruins of these industries can be seen along this route. The rocky shores of the river were scraped bare by glaciation eons ago; potholes were gouged out of the granite by swirling water and rocks. White marble outcrops add to the geological beauty at several points. Cottages frequently dot this route.

The Mississippi can be a dangerous river; only expert canoeists are advised to travel this route in spring. In summer the river is often quite low, requiring more portaging and lining. Drinking water should be treated. Below Crotch Lake most portages are on private land and, in many cases, not marked by signs. Fishing: pickerel, pike, bass, lake trout.

Route (97) Charleston Lake-Gananoque Lake Loop

Type Lake and river route

Rating B C C C

Length 53 km / 2 days

Portages 2

Main bodies of water Charleston and Gananoque Lakes

Start / Finish Charleston Lake Provincial Park by road (off Hwy 3) or Outlet by road (Hwy 3)

Traversing an area rich in Indian history, this route offers numerous glimpses of the native culture. There are prehistoric rock shelters along the steep, rugged shoreline of Charleston Lake and an impressive pictograph on Red Horse Lake. One explanation of the name Tallow Rock Bay is that Indians made tallow on this site; some say the smell can still be detected on the rocks. The soft, white rock nearby is another possible origin of the name. Other points of interest include Wiltse Marsh, one of the largest cattail marshes in the area and home to blue herons, American bitterns, redwing blackbirds, ducks and coots. Much of this route goes through a rocky, white pine and hardwood landscape typical of Shield topography usually found farther north. Cottage development is interspersed with long uninhabited stretches.

Charleston Lake should not be canoed in high winds or stormy weather. The dam at Outlet can affect water level and velocity. Drinking water should be treated. Fishing: lake trout, bass, pike, panfish.

Detailed information *Pine Trees and Portages: A Mississippi Canoeing Experience*

Source Mississippi Valley Conservation Authority, Box 419, Carleton Place, Ontario K7C 3P5

Detailed information *Charleston Lake-Gananoque Lake Canoe Route*

Source Ministry of Natural Resources, 101 Water Street, Brockville, Ontario K6V 5Y8

Route (98) Nottawasaga River

Type River route

Rating B n/a C C

Length 120 km / 3 days

Portages 5

Main bodies of water Nottawasaga River, Jack Lake

Start Hockley Valley by road (Airport Road at Hockley Valley Road)

Finish Wasaga Beach by road (Hwy 92)

Intermediate access Numerous points by road

From Hockley Valley to Angus the Nottawasaga River offers exciting springtime canoeing, scenic landscape and excellent trout fishing. Flowing northward over the Nicolston dam, the river is joined by major tributaries from the sand plains to the east and the Niagara Escarpment to the west. Between Angus and Edenvale the river bisects the forested Minesing Swamp, one of the largest wetland systems in southern Ontario. The hackberry tree, a Carolinian forest species which normally does not grow this far north, can be found along this section. The swamp is also a popular stopover during bird migrations, and waterfowl abound in spring and autumn, with many staying to nest in the area. This section is recommended for springtime canoeing only because low water may cause problems with numerous deadheads and liftovers. From Edenvale to Wasaga Beach the river is slow and meandering, suitable for novice canoeists throughout the season. Along this section the river flows through a central valley of the Edenvale moraine and past the largest group of parabolic sand dunes in the province. Jack Lake, a remnant of a post-glacial lagoon behind the dunes, is also of interest. Once a major travelling artery for native people, explorers and fur traders, this route offers historic and military sites (Schooner Town, Van Vlack and Nancy Island) along the populated stretches near the mouth of the river. Except for the Wasaga Beach section, the route is almost exclusively rural.

Because of nearly nonexistent camping facilities, this route is best for day trips only. Above Edenvale the river can be canoed only during spring runoff. Canoeists planning to explore the Minesing Swamp are advised to use compass and map, for there are no fences or roads to follow once the river is left behind. Insects are also a problem in this area. The Nottawasaga River develops strong currents near its mouth, and canoeists should expect heavy motorboat travel on the approach to Wasaga Beach. The river appears muddy because of the burden of silt and sand it carries. Almost all lands along the river are privately owned, and permission must be requested before camping. Fishing: pike, pickerel, rainbow trout.

Detailed information *Guide to the Nottawasaga Valley Conservation Authority*
Source Nottawasaga Valley Conservation Authority, R.R.1, Angus, Ontario L0M 1B0
Detailed information *Canoeing the Nottawasaga.* (This brochure describes the Edenvale-to-Wasaga Beach section.)
Source Ministry of Natural Resources, Midhurst, Ontario L0L 1X0

Route (99) Beaver River

Type River route

Rating A n/a C C

Length 27 km / 1 to 2 days

Portages 3

Main bodies of water Beaver River

Start Kimberley by road (off Hwy 4)

Finish Thornbury by road (Hwy 26)

Intermediate access Several points by road

Cutting through the deep, glaciated Beaver Valley, the Beaver River route is one of the most scenic canoe trips in southern Ontario. The variety of landscapes includes farm land, flooded forests, hardwood stands and views of the craggy limestone cliffs of the Niagara Escarpment. The upper section, from Kimberley to Heathcote, winds over poorly drained bottomlands. Below Heathcote the gradient becomes rather steep, and the river develops many sets of rapids that can provide challenging whitewater canoeing in high water. Although the river has had its mill and logging days, subsequent land use has not been intensive, and much of this route appears in its natural state.

Since the route is intended for day use, campsites are not provided. However, Craigleith Provincial Park is nearby. Water is not drinkable. The Heathcote-to-Thornbury stretch is passable only in the spring. Fishing: brown trout, rainbow trout.

Detailed information *Beaver River Canoe Route*
Source Ministry of Natural Resources, 611 Ninth Avenue East, Owen Sound, Ontario N4K 3E4
or
North Grey Region Conservation Authority, Box 759, Owen Sound, Ontario N4K 5W9

Route (100) Rankin River

Type River and lake route

Rating B B C C

Length 18 km / 1 day

Portages 3

Main bodies of water Isaac and Boat Lakes, Rankin River

Start Sky Lake by road (left at Mar off Hwy 6)

Finish Sauble Falls by road (off Hwy 21)

Intermediate access Between Isaac and Boat Lakes off Hwy 6

The slow-moving Rankin River was used for hundreds of years by Indians crossing the base of the Bruce Peninsula. The flat area through which the river flows was once a prehistoric lake bottom, and the sand dunes to the west of the river mark the ancient shoreline. Today, drowned forest, the result of a water control dam on the lower Rankin River, dominates the landscape. But this forest and the shallow, marshy lakes that are connected by the river provide excellent opportunities for wildlife viewing. Aquatic plants, such as pickerel weed and fragrant water lily, flourish here, and black ash and silver maple are established in some sections. Downstream from the control dam are two sets of rapids that must be portaged in times of low water. Also in the lower reaches of the Rankin River are several saw logs visible along the river bottom.

Water is not drinkable. The shallow lakes tend to become weed-covered in sections by late summer. Campsites are available at Sauble Falls Provincial Park. Fishing: pike, bass, pickerel, perch.

Route (101) Saugeen River

Type River route

Rating B n/a C C

Length 92 km / 2 to 3 days

Portages 4

Main body of water Saugeen River

Start Hanover Park by road (Hwy 4)

Finish Denny's Dam, Southampton by road (Hwy 21)

Intermediate access Walkerton by road (Hwy 4), Paisley by road (County Road 3)

The Saugeen River rises in one of the highest points in southwestern Ontario and flows through scenic rolling countryside to Lake Huron. Passing through heavy mixed forest interspersed with pasture land, this route was used in the 1850s by pioneers settling in Bruce County. River conditions vary from broad, placid sections to stretches with rapids and eddies, making the route ideal for both family trips and the novice fastwater canoeist. Glacial-fluvial features include river terraces, thirty-metre sand and clay bluffs, spillways and a former delta area.

Provisions and campsites are available in towns along the way. Water is not drinkable. Low water in late summer may make sections of the river impassable. Rapids can be difficult in early spring. Fishing: bass, pike, brown trout, rainbow trout.

Detailed information *Rankin River Canoe Route*

Source Ministry of Natural Resources,
611 Ninth Avenue East, Owen Sound, Ontario N4K 3E4
or
Sauble Valley Conservation Authority,
Box 759, Owen Sound, Ontario N4K 5W9

Detailed information *Saugeen River Canoe Route*

Source Ministry of Natural Resources,
611 Ninth Avenue East, Owen Sound, Ontario N4K 3E4
or
Saugeen Valley Conservation Authority,
R.R. 1, Hanover, Ontario N4N 3B8

Route (102) Maitland River

Type River route

Rating B n/a C C

Length 100 km / 2 to 3 days

Portages 3

Main body of water Maitland River

Start Wroxeter by road (Hwy 87)

Finish Goderich by road (Hwys 8 and 21)

Intermediate access Wingham by road (Hwys 4 and 86), Auburn by road (off Hwy 4)

Extensive farm lands dominate the landscape at the start of this route, but the river soon enters a deep valley of the Wyoming Spillway, which screens the surrounding fields. The Maitland River meanders through shallow, gravelly channels and swamps between Wroxeter and Wingham. Below Wingham and Holmesville the canoeist finds alternating stretches of quiet water and rapids. Flowing north from Holmesville, the river cuts through a section of the valley displaying magnificent examples of incised meanders. The trip ends within a kilometre of Lake Huron, where the valley is fifty metres deep with steep banks.

Water levels are suitable for canoeing the entire route only in the early spring. The Wingham-to-Auburn section can be travelled from spring until fall. Campsites are available at parks and private campgrounds in the area. Canoeists should watch for barbed wire fences across the river. Fishing: pike, bass, rainbow trout, brown trout, migrant salmon.

Route (103) Bayfield River

Type River route

Rating C n/a n/a C

Length 40 km / 1 day

Portages 0

Main body of water Bayfield River

Start Egmondville by road (off County Road 12)

Finish Bayfield by road (Hwy 21)

Intermediate access Varna by road (off Hwy 4), Clinton by road (Hwys 4 and 8)

The Bayfield River begins as a small, winding stream and grows into a wide, fast river, which cuts through a deep gorge just before entering Lake Huron. White water enlivens some points on the river. Prior to the arrival of the Canada Company in 1827, the Bayfield watershed was controlled by Ojibway Indians; it is presently devoted to cattle farming.

The Bayfield River should be canoed only during the spring runoff in April and May. Campsites are available at Bayfield. Fishing: pike, bass, rainbow trout, brown trout, migrant salmon.

Detailed information *Canoe the Maitland*

Source Ministry of Natural Resources, R.R. 5, Wingham, Ontario N0G 2W0

Detailed information *Canoe the Bayfield River*

Source Ministry of Natural Resources, R.R. 5, Wingham, Ontario N0G 2W0

Route (104) Lower Thames River

Type River route

Rating B n/a n/a C

Length 144 km / 4 to 7 days

Portages 0

Main body of water Thames River

Start Delaware by road (Hwy 2)

Finish Chatham by road (Hwy 2)

Intermediate access Big Bend Conservation Area by road (off Hwy 2)

Between Delaware and Thamesville the Thames River drops at a fairly constant rate to form swifts and rapids. Rich in native history, the river flows through three Indian reserves along this route. Points of interest include a privately owned bird sanctuary, an old mill site and cairns commemorating the 1814 Battle of the Longwoods and the death of the great Shawnee chief, Tecumseh. Once an important source of power and transportation, the lower stretches of the river retained their economic importance to the region as a route for lake freighters. Today, commercial traffic has been replaced by recreational boating. A series of pools and rapids marks the stretch between Delaware and Muncey Bridge, with numerous rocks just below the surface. Downstream from Muncey Bridge shallows and shoals are common. This route travels through three conservation areas, two public parks and several towns.

The majority of suitable camping spots are located on private property; permission must be asked before using them. River water is not drinkable, and drinking water should be obtained from a safe source. Though this trip can be extended thirty kilometres from Chatham to Lake St. Clair, that stretch is not recommended for canoeists. The river becomes very slow and sluggish and is used extensively by motorboats. Fishing: pickerel, carp, perch, bass.

Route (105) Big Creek

Type River route

Rating C n/a n/a C

Length 40 km / 1 to 2 days

Portages 0

Main body of water Big Creek

Start Delhi by road (Hwy 3)

Finish Long Point by road (Hwy 59)

Intermediate access Wherever a township road crosses the creek

Big Creek has cut deeply into the surrounding farm lands of the Norfolk Sand Plain, leaving a valley that is more than thirty metres deep in places. The creek flows cold and clear from March to December. Many Carolinian forest species can be seen along the creek, and deer, muskrat, Canada geese and wood duck live in the area. In the past Big Creek has been important as a source of power for local grist, flour and saw mills.

During periods of drought low water levels may make canoeing difficult. There are no campsites along the route, and all land bordering the creek is privately owned. Fishing: rainbow trout, brook trout, brown trout.

Detailed information *Canoe the Lower Thames River*

Source Lower Thames Valley Conservation Authority, 41 Fourth Street, Chatham, Ontario N7M 2G3

Detailed information *Big Creek Canoe Route*

Source Ministry of Natural Resources, 645 Norfolk Street North, Simcoe, Ontario N3Y 3R2

Route (106) Grand River

Type River route

Rating C C C C

Length 150 km / 4 to 6 days

Portages 13

Main bodies of water Lake Belwood, Grand River

Start Lake Belwood by road (north of Hwy 6)

Finish Port Maitland by road (south of Hwy 3)

Intermediate access Many points by road

Before the arrival of the Europeans this warm, turbid river carried many native tribes, including the Hurons, Neutrals, Tobaccos and Iroquois, on their war and trading expeditions. The valley of the Grand was given to the Six Nations Iroquois in return for their support of the Crown during the American Revolution. However, the area soon passed into the hands of white entrepreneurs, and its development was swift. Though the Grand River today traverses populated agricultural and urban areas, its heavily wooded banks with their abundant wildlife recall the river as it once was. The Elora Gorge section should not be canoed, but its sculpted walls are worth exploring. An ideal waterway for day trips, the Grand River passes by many historic attractions, including the picturesque town of Paris, the Six Nations Reserve, the home of poet Pauline Johnson and remnants of the canal and lock system that once carried the lake boats upriver to Brantford from the Erie Canal.

Though some sections of the Grand River are deep and slow-moving, others become rather shallow in the summer, and it is sometimes necessary to wade canoes through. Campsites are located in a few Conservation Authority parks and commercial facilities, but it is usually possible to find good camping spots on the riverbank, providing permission is requested from property owners. Drinking water should be treated. Fishing: bass, pike, perch, carp, catfish, bullhead; coho salmon below Caledonia.

Route (107) Welland River

Type River route

Rating C C C C

Length 115 km / 4 to 5 days

Portages 2

Main bodies of water Lake Niapenco, Welland River

Start Binbrook Conservation Area by road (Hwy 56)

Finish Chippawa by road (Niagara Parkway)

Intermediate access Many points by road

This meandering, often sluggish waterway makes its way through agricultural lands in its upper reaches and descends into more urban and industrial areas. Once an important shipping artery, the river formed part of the earliest Welland Canal system.

Much of the river flows through private property, and permission must be requested to camp on the riverbank. Other campsites can be found in Conservation Authority parks and commercial facilities; but these are distributed unevenly, and canoeists are advised to plan ahead before setting out on a trip of more than one day. In fact, the Welland is an ideal river for day trips, thanks to the numerous access points along this route. The Lake Niapenco-to-Port Davidson section is suitable for canoeing only in early spring. The water is not drinkable. Fishing: pike, panfish.

Detailed information *Canoeing on the Grand*

Source Ministry of Natural Resources,
R.R. 1, Beaverdale Road, Cambridge, Ontario N3C 2V3

Detailed information *Canoeing the Welland River*

Source Ministry of Natural Resources,
Box 1070, Fonthill, Ontario L0S 1E0

Area (Q) Killarney Provincial Park

Type Lake routes

Length 5 documented routes / 30 to 90 km / 2 to 7 days

Main bodies of water George, Killarney, O.S.A., Threenarrows, Nellie and David Lakes

Access George Lake campground by road (Hwy 637)

Killarney Provincial Park is famous for its white quartzite mountains dotted with scrub oak, stunted pine and maple. Its crystal-clear lakes are tinged an unusual turquoise blue. Several of these waterways were used by fur traders to bypass rough water on Georgian Bay. In later years logs were driven through the area to the Bay, and old chutes and dams can still be found within the park. The beauty of this area was celebrated by the Group of Seven, whose efforts led to the creation of the park to preserve this expanse of wilderness for future generations. Canoeing in Killarney consists primarily of lake paddling, with connecting portages of varying difficulty and length. There is very little river paddling and virtually no white water here. Canoeists can set out on foot from their shoreline camps and climb above the maple and birch bush to the quartzite ridges with their breathtaking views. One point, Silver Peak, towers over 300 metres above the surrounding lakes.

The detail provided by the park map will enable canoeists to plan their own routes. O.S.A. and Killarney Lakes are the most popular, but a willingness to cross difficult portages into Threenarrows Lake permits exploration of a relatively untravelled and equally scenic part of the park. Although most lakes are devoid of game fish, thanks to the effects of acid rain, pike, bass and pickerel can be found in Threenarrows Lake.

Area (R) Algonquin Provincial Park

Type Lake routes

Length Numerous routes possible / 10 to 500 km / 1 to 28 days

Main bodies of water Over 1500 lakes and rivers comprising the headwaters of the Petawawa, Opeongo, Bonnechere, Madawaska, Oxtongue and Amable du Fond Rivers

Access Twenty-nine points by road in and around the park

The oldest of Ontario's provincial parks, Algonquin offers a superb wilderness experience within easy driving distance of the province's major population centres. In operation since 1893, the park today is world-reknowned for its scenic, scientific and recreational resources. The western two-thirds of the park are covered mainly in southern hardwoods. Here, on elevations of ancient Shield bedrock, five rivers have their headwaters. The eastern section of the park is lower, and in this area sandier, drier soils promote the growth of the red, white and jack pine that attracted nineteenth-century loggers. The legendary beauty of the park has been captured by artists such as Tom Thomson, who drowned under mysterious circumstances on Canoe Lake. A web of over 1600 kilometres of interconnecting waterways, this area features small and medium-size lakes and generally slow-moving stretches of river. Campsites are well distributed, and the well-cleared portages average 500 metres in length. There is little white water here. A series of hiking and nature trails is available to canoeists who want to stretch their land legs. There is virtually no permanent settlement in the area and very few signs of man's presence.

Low water in some creeks and rivers may pose problems late in the season. Fishing: lake trout, brook trout, smallmouth bass.

Detailed information *Killarney Provincial Park Map* ($1.00 plus sales tax)

Source Ministry of Natural Resources, Box 3500, Station A, Sudbury, Ontario P3A 4S2

Detailed information *Algonquin Provincial Park Canoe Routes* ($1.00)

Source Ministry of Natural Resources, Box 219, Whitney, Ontario K0J 2M0

Area (S) Gull River

Type Lake and river routes

Length 5 documented routes / 10 to 86 km / 1 to 3 days

Main bodies of water Gull River, Shadow, Moore, Gull, Twelve Mile, Kushog, Redstone, Kennisis and Kawagama Lakes

Access Buttermilk Falls by road (Hwy 35), Kennisis Lake Dam by road (off Hwy 530)

The Gull River system once carried Indians into the rich hunting grounds of the Algonquin Park region and later transported timber during nineteenth-century log drives. A log chute at the Elliott Falls dam, dating back to the mid 1800s, was restored in 1975. Also on that site stands a powerhouse that operated between 1903 and 1928 to service the villages of Kirkfield and Victoria Road. The routes in this area travel through a typical Canadian Shield landscape with rock cliffs and frequent waterfalls. Kennisis, Boshkung and Twelve Mile Lakes boast some of the best lake trout fishing in the area.

No public land is available for campsites, and permission must be requested before camping. Many side trips can be added to the main travel routes. Most of the lakes and portions of the river are dotted with cottages, and motorboats are common in the summer. One of the described routes is a circular trip. Fishing: lake trout, brook trout, rainbow trout, muskellunge, smallmouth bass, largemouth bass.

Area (T) North Kawartha

Type Lake and river routes

Length 5 documented routes / 13 to 48 km / 1 to 3 days

Main bodies of water Catchacoma, Mississagua, Anstruther, Stony, Lovesick and Lower Buckhorn Lakes, Mississagua River

Access Numerous points by road via Hwys 28 and 507

The North Kawartha routes are located within the Burleigh-Harvey Recreation Zone on the southern edge of the Canadian Shield. The reserve includes forested land, swamp-filled depressions, open woodland and rock barrens. A large fire in 1913 burned over most of this area, and the present mixed conifer-hardwood forest is a result of limited regrowth. The suggested routes follow numerous lakes and streams draining southwest into the Trent-Severn Canal System and, with the exception of the Mississagua River trip, can be travelled in either direction. Longer trips can be developed by linking routes together. At High Falls on Eels Creek, a popular and scenic camping area, the Ministry of Natural Resources maintains a hiking trail to Petroglyphs Provincial Park. The park contains one of the largest single concentrations of prehistoric rock art in Canada, artifacts of Algonquin-speaking people who lived in the region at least 1000 years ago. More recent relics in this area include remains of the early timber industry. Once a major log-driving river, the Mississagua is strewn with ruins of stone and timber dams and timber slides. Animal attractions include deer and black bear. The large lakes in this area have been developed intensively, but development is minimal away from the larger bodies of water.

Individual canoeing skills will determine what sections of the Mississagua River and Eels Creek must be portaged. The Trent-Severn Canal System and the large lakes are used frequently by motorboats. Water levels remain constant throughout the summer, except for the Mississagua River, which is controlled by a dam at the outlet of Mississagua Lake. Drinking water should be treated. Fishing: smallmouth bass, largemouth bass, lake trout, brook trout, rainbow trout, muskellunge.

Detailed information *Gull River Canoe Routes*

Source Ministry of Natural Resources, Minden, Ontario K0M 2K0

Detailed information *North Kawartha Canoe Routes* and *High Falls Hiking Trail*

Source Ministry of Natural Resources, Box 500, Bancroft, Ontario K0L 1C0
or
Ministry of Natural Resources, Minden, Ontario K0M 2K0

Area (U) Cataraqui

Type Lake and river routes

Length 8 documented routes / 19 to 96 km / 1 to 4 days

Main bodies of water Rideau, Newboro, Opinicon, Sand, Lower Beverley, Charleston and Loughborough Lakes, Rideau Canal, Gananoque River

Access Many points by road off Hwys 15, 32 and 42

These routes traverse a southern extension of the Canadian Shield known as the Frontenac Axis, a granite-based upland laced with many lakes and rivers draining mainly into the St. Lawrence River. Once extremely rich in game, the mixed deciduous and coniferous forests of the Frontenac Axis were favourite seasonal hunting grounds for native peoples. In the late 1820s a section of the Rideau Canal, connecting Ottawa and Kingston, was built through this area to provide a communications and supply line that could not be cut easily by the Americans. The locks of the canal are still in working order. A great number of white pine were taken off the Frontenac Axis near the turn of the century, and the lumberjacks were followed by cottagers, who have made the area a favourite to this day. Most canoeing here is lake paddling, with short portages around locks and dams.

Much of the land abutting these routes is privately owned, and permission must be requested from the owners before camping. Camp wherever possible at designated campsites. Beware of motorboat traffic and of winds on the larger lakes. Drinking water should be treated. Fishing: lake trout, bass, pike, panfish.

Detailed information

Route 2-72 (Chaffeys Locks Loop)
96 km / 3 to 4 days / 4 portages
This route, which circles Opinicon and Sand Lakes, can easily be broken into smaller trips or extended with side trips.

Route 1A-76 (Newboro Loop)
26 km / 1 day / no portages
This route circles Upper Rideau Lake, which can be dangerous in high winds. Of interest is the Foley Mountain Conservation Area, with its panoramic views and nature trails. At Narrows Lock one of the blockhouses built for the defence of the Rideau Canal has been restored.

Route 1-71 (Newboro Loop)
32 km / 1 to 2 days / no portages
This route circles Newboro, Indian and Clear Lakes.

Route 7-77 (Perth Road Loop)
40 km / 2 days / no portages
This route circles Loughborough Lake and reaches some relatively uninhabited parts.

Route 4A-74 (Delta to Charleston)
27 km / 2 days / 2 portages
This route follows Lindhurst Creek and several small lakes to Charleston Lake.

Route 4-72 (Delta to St. Lawrence River)
96 km / 3 to 4 days / 2 portages
This route offers mainly river paddling. It follows Lindhurst Creek to the Gananoque River, then downriver to the St. Lawrence.

Route 3-73 (Jones Falls to Delta)
19 km / 1 day / 1 portage
The Horseshoe Dam, constructed in 1831 at Jones Falls, was considered an engineering masterpiece of its time.

Route 5-70 (Seeleys Bay Loop)
19 km / 1 day / no portages
This route circles Whitefish Lake around Deans Island.

Source Cataraqui Region Conservation Authority, R.R.1, Glenburnie, Ontario K0H 1S0

Canoe Trip Safety

Each year many canoeists encounter difficulties because of an unrealistic appraisal of their own abilities and equipment and a disregard for the powers of nature. Such errors in judgement can cause serious injury or even loss of life.

The following safety tips emphasize key aspects of canoe safety. Take heed of them, for in the long run *you* are responsible for your own well-being.

1 Never attempt a trip that will overtax your ability. Improve your skill by meeting progressively stiffer challenges, but do so gradually and, if possible, under the guidance of an expert.

2 *Every canoeist should know how to swim.* You should feel comfortable in the water and practice swimming while wearing your PFD (personal flotation device). You should also know how to give mouth-to-mouth resuscitation.

The law requires that there be one PFD for each person in a canoe. You should wear your PFD at all times.

3 Be especially careful when canoeing on cold water. Hypothermia is a constant danger if you fall in. In essence, hypothermia is a lowering of the core body temperature to a level where normal thinking and acting become impossible. Death can result, either as a direct result of chilling or, more often, from drowning. Hypothermia can also be caused by exhaustion and chilling in damp, cold conditions: You need not fall in the water at all.

The first symptom of hypothermia is shivering that grows increasingly more violent and uncontrollable. It is followed by vague, slow speech, memory loss and incoherence. The victim may experience loss of coordination in hands and legs, drowsiness, exhaustion and, finally, coma.

As a guard against the dangerous effects of hypothermia, always wear your PFD. Hypothermia can render even a good swimmer helpless in minutes. If you cannot get out of the water immediately, get some clothing on: a hat, coat or even raingear. These can prevent heat loss in the water.

To treat hypothermia, get the victim out of the water, out of the weather, out of wet clothes. Put him or her into dry clothes and into a warm sleeping bag. Give hot drinks. *Never give alcohol or tobacco to a hypothermia victim;* these draw warmth away from the core of the body.

If the victim is in a severe state of hypothermia and is semiconscious, try to keep him or her awake. In this case remove the victim's clothing and put him or her into a warm sleeping bag with another person, also stripped. Build a fire.

Remember, hypothermia is a leading cause of canoeing deaths.

4 You should always have an extra paddle and a bailer (a tin can or plastic container tied to the canoe so it will not be lost).

For overnight trips you should take a complete change of clothes stored in a waterproof bag, extra food in case of forced delays and a personal survival kit to be carried by each member of the party. The kit should include items such as waterproof matches, fishing line, hooks, a knife and compass. A duplicate set of maps, tucked away in a safe place, is also recommended. Anything in the canoe that could be damaged by a soaking (sleeping bags, food) should be kept in waterproof bags or containers.

Carry a complete first aid kit and know how to use it to treat burns, cuts and broken bones. When any emergency strikes, stay calm. If someone is injured, decide whether he or she is best moved to the nearest settlement or tended in the bush.

5 The standard SOS call in wilderness areas is a series of three signals of any kind, either audible or visual. A smudge fire can be used to alert passing aircraft; an SOS composed of letters at least three metres high can be laid on the ground.

20 *The proper loading of a canoe
ensures good balance and ready access
to the most frequently used gear.*

21 *Some canoeists fail to appreciate the
powers of nature until it is too late.*

20

21

6 In remote areas it is not a good idea to canoe alone. An injury or loss of canoe can spell disaster. Parties of two or three canoes (two people per canoe) are recommended. However, larger parties are discouraged because they place too much stress on campsites. (See Low-Impact Canoe Camping, "The Campsite", page 104.)

7 Know your route well beforehand. Estimate its challenges accurately and prepare accordingly. Use detailed topographic maps and know your position on them at all times. Alternate access points (roads, railways, other waterways) should be noted beforehand in case an emergency means the trip must be shortened.

8 For your own safety *please* note that canoe travel north of the 50th parallel is serious business. If you have not tried it before, seriously consider taking your first trip in that region in the company of an experienced guide. At the *minimum*, travel with someone who has already canoed there. Remember, the climate is harsh, rivers are large and unforgiving, and help is rarely available. Maps and brochures provided by the Ministry of Natural Resources for northern rivers *must* be supplemented by experience. Heed this advice; it may save your life.

9 Rivers and lakes change in character from season to season and year to year. Conditions may not always correspond to those described on maps and brochures. For example, a section of river that is a violent rapids in June may become a maze of rocks by August. A rapids that another canoeist describes to you as "easy" may have appeared so only because he was more skilled than you or luckier than he realized.

On rivers where water levels are controlled by dams, beware of camping and storing canoes on shores that may be flooded in the night. It pays to check water levels with local offices of the Ministry of Natural Resources and/or Conservation Authorities.

10 The decision to run a rapids can have serious consequences: loss of equipment, loss of canoe, loss of life. The majority of rapids have portages. Unless absolutely sure of your ability to run a given rapids, use the portage.

Never paddle into a rapids without surveying it first from shore. If you must line or wade a canoe through rapids, you can avoid being swept off your feet by never wading in deeper than knee height. Always wear your PFD.

11 Open water can be very dangerous, especially larger lakes and river mouths where winds can generate large waves in thirty minutes or less. Stay close to shore wherever possible and learn to choose protected channels behind islands. It is not a mark of cowardice to stop on shore if waves make travel difficult. Even the voyageurs did this.

12 An improperly used axe can cause serious injury. Keep axes, saws and knives properly sheathed when not in use. Short-handled axes are far more dangerous than long-handled ones. If you miss striking the wood with a long-handled axe, chances are the head will bury itself in the ground. A short-handled one may bury itself in you. A portable saw (there are lightweight, folding varieties) is safer and easier to use.

A portable stove is highly recommended as an excellent way of getting around the bother and danger of cutting wood.

13 Animals very rarely cause injuries to human beings; however, they can cause problems with food supplies. Since animals are attracted to campsites by the smell of food and garbage, it is important to keep your site as clean and odour-free as possible. Never bury garbage; animals will detect it and dig it up. Keep all food wrapped in plastic to reduce odours. Place the wrapped food in a pack and, using a rope, suspend it from a tree branch at least three metres above the ground and two metres out from the trunk. Do not hang it near your tent, and *never* keep food in your tent or under your canoe: Bears go *through* objects not around them.

Never clean fish in the vicinity of your camp since the odour may attract bears. If a bear does appear, retreat quietly without turning your back on the animal. If it sees you, do not crouch low: This is sometimes taken as an invitation to attack. Bears are particularly dangerous in spring, when they are protective of their cubs.

Never feed any wild animal. If an animal is accustomed to receiving "handouts", it will lose its fear of people and become a nuisance to other campers. Because of the thoughtless acts of some people, many of these "tame" animals have had to be destroyed.

14 Mosquitoes and black flies are active during most of the canoeing season. They are at their worst from late May through June and then tend to decrease gradually in number. Your best protection is proper clothing. Wear long-sleeved shirts and tuck pantlegs inside heavy wool socks or boot tops. A hat provides excellent protection from deerflies and horseflies, which flourish later in the summer. Wear light-coloured clothing and avoid dark colours (especially blues and greens), which tend to attract insects. Insect repellents are also very useful, and screened tents are essential for restful sleep during mosquito season.

15 Sunburn and glare can cause serious discomfort. Seasoned canoeists wear wide-brimmed hats, long-sleeved shirts and sunglasses. Some even wear cotton gardening gloves to protect the backs of their hands. A bandanna is also helpful. Be sure to take a bottle or two of screening lotion and some lip salve.

16 Pay special attention to drinking water. In many instances the water is pure and fit to drink, but not always. Why take chances when precautions are so simple? Many canoeists treat water from *all* sources. Downstream from any settlement or industry, drinking water should always be treated either by chemical means, such as purification tablets, iodine or Javex, or by boiling. When water is taken from beaver ponds, the only safe method of treatment is boiling for fifteen minutes to kill parasitic organisms that may be present.

17 Canoeing offers a kind of freedom not readily found in our day-to-day life. However, it also places a demand for self-reliance on the canoeist. In the final analysis *you are responsible for your own safety.*

In emergencies help is usually far away. You must be prepared to avoid potential dangers *before* accidents happen. You must also know how to cope with emergencies when they do occur. In short, know your equipment, your abilities, your companions and yourself.

Groups often ignore the importance of leadership on a canoe trip. This lack of foresight can lead to personal conflicts and/or breakdown of the group when cooperation is most essential. Areas of responsibility should be decided for all members of the group before the trip begins. In some instances it is appropriate for one person to make all decisions and allocate tasks. In others duties can be shared. For example, one person can be "camp boss" (chief cook); another can navigate and captain the group when on the water. The organization will depend on individual skills and the nature of the group. Make sure the members of your group establish a working relationship before you set out. It will contribute to both your safety and enjoyment of the trip.

22

Low-Impact Canoe Camping

23

24

Respect your environment. Nurture it and it will continue to provide you and others with an experience of inestimable value. Even though you may encounter few, if any, other canoeists, remember that your route may be travelled by many others at different times and that the cumulative impact of many thoughtless users can destroy the beauty and life of the water and land.

Your passage through wilderness areas should leave no trace. The following guidelines will help you accomplish this goal.

The Campsite
1 Keep your group size relatively small (six or less). A large group may necessitate expansion of existing sites, with the result that trees and ground cover are destroyed.

2 Use existing campsites, trails and portages. Do not camp on the ends of portages in heavily used areas, as this obstructs the progress of others along the trail. Do not stay too long in one place, as this tends to wear out a campsite.

3 Do not cut live trees or shrubs to make shelters or tent poles. Use a self-supporting tent. Never strip live bark from trees.

4 Do not dig drainage trenches around your tent. Trenches scar the site, accelerate erosion and make things awkward for others. Ever tried sleeping in a trench? Take advantage of natural drainage and use a floored tent.

Fires
1 Use lightweight camp stoves in place of fires for cooking. These stoves are convenient to use in all weather, present a minimal fire hazard and are much cleaner and faster than fires. They also do away with the necessity of collecting and chopping wood.

2 If you must have a fire, remember that restricted travel zones are sometimes declared as a result of dangerous forest fire conditions. Check with the nearest Ministry of Natural Resources district office before starting your

trip to see whether a travel permit is required. Anyone convicted of starting a forest fire can be charged with the expense of fighting that fire under the laws of Ontario.

3 Use only dead wood for your fire. On small islands do not collect firewood; repeated searching over a small area soon destroys the vegetation. Gather your firewood along the shore of the mainland and large islands. For most purposes wood need not be thicker than your thumb.

4 Keep fires small and build them in existing fire pits. If the area is untravelled, remove evidence of fire after use. Where there is no fire pit, dig to the mineral level of the soil, avoiding the burnable soil, roots and overhanging trees.

5 To extinguish the fire, let it burn out to a white ash. Retrieve non-burnables, such as foil, tin cans, plastics and glass, and carry them out with you. Douse the fire thoroughly. Stir the ashes and the area surrounding the ashes. Douse again. If you cannot touch the ashes, do not consider the fire out.

Human Waste
1 Use existing outhouses. Otherwise, bury human waste in a small, shallow latrine at least 100 metres away from the water. Make sure the waste is in the upper, biologically active layer of the soil, where bacteria can decompose it.

2 Use single-ply, white toilet paper and bury it completely. Some people prefer to collect the paper and burn it.

Other Waste
1 What is carried in must also be carried out. Burn it, bash it, bag it, bring it back.

2 Wash dishes, clothes and yourself in a dishpan, not in the lake or river. Rinse away from the open water. Dump dirty water at least fifty metres from the shoreline. Use biodegradable soap.

3 Whenever you can, clean up the mess left by careless campers who have gone before you. Inform the author-

25 *Lunch break. Wisely, the food is being kept in waterproof bags and unbreakable, reusable containers.*

27 *Two that got away.*

26 *A canoeist beaches his craft after a day's paddle.*

25

26

ities of the mistakes of others if they are too extensive for you to correct. Leave the site cleaner than you find it.

Wildlife and Natural Foods

1 Ontario residents do not require fishing licenses. Non-residents of Ontario may purchase fishing licenses from any district office of the Ministry of Natural Resources, its Public Service Centre in Toronto, some sporting goods stores, most lodges and the park offices at Algonquin and Quetico Provincial Parks. Information on seasons and catch limits is contained in the Ontario *Summary of Fishing Regulations,* which can be obtained from the above-mentioned sources or from the Parks and Recreational Areas Branch or Fisheries Branch of the Ministry of Natural Resources. (See Sources of Further Information, page 107.)

2 Do not plan to live off the land by hunting on your canoe trips. Firearms are prohibited in most provincial parks, and hunting is regulated by the Game and Fish Act, which states that hunting licenses are not valid

during the months of July and August for most game. The possession of a firearm in any area inhabited by game is prima facie evidence of hunting. (Firearms also include air or pellet guns, longbows and crossbows.) Check the *Summary of Hunting Regulations* for further details. (See Sources of Further Information, page 107.)

3 Removal of or damage to any plant, shrub, tree or flower within a provincial park is specifically prohibited by law, and the practice is discouraged elsewhere.

Landowner Relations

Some canoe routes, especially in southern Ontario, run past private land. Naturally, the utmost courtesy should be exercised:
Stay on portages.
Ask permission before camping on private land.
Use only those campsites indicated on the map or posted with a sign.
Leave no trace behind.
If you break trust with the landowner, he or she may withdraw canoeing privileges for others.

27

Sources of Further Information

The following list of recommended sources touches all aspects of canoeing, from planning your trip to conducting it enjoyably and safely. The list is by no means exhaustive; for more information on specific topics contact your local bookstore or library.

Major Canoeing Organizations
Canoe Ontario represents the interests of canoeists and kayakers, racing and recreational canoeing clubs, canoe camps and guides. It promotes marathon canoe racing, flatwater (Olympic-style) racing and whitewater racing. It also trains leaders for canoe tripping and takes a keen interest in environmental issues affecting canoeists. This organization can direct you to instruction in all styles of canoeing, to canoeing and kayaking clubs and to camps that specialize in canoe tripping. Memberships in Canoe Ontario are available to those interested in receiving the organization's wide range of publications and services. Contact
Canoe Ontario
160 Vanderhoof Avenue
Toronto, Ontario M4G 4B8
Phone 416-429-7701.

Travel Information
Roads
For commercial bus operations see your local travel agent. For a free official road map of Ontario write
Ontario Travel
Queen's Park
Toronto, Ontario M7A 2E5
Phone 416-965-4008.

Rail
The passenger services of the Canadian National and Canadian Pacific Railways have been combined under the name Via Rail. Via Rail will drop off canoes and pick them up at remote locations if the train in question includes a full-size baggage car and if space is available. There is a six-metre limit on canoes, and only one is allowed per person. For information about fees, schedules and reservations contact
Via Rail Passenger Reservation and Information
Fifth Floor, 20 King Street West
Toronto, Ontario M5H 1C4
Phone 416-366-8411.

The Algoma Central Railway, which runs north out of Sault Ste. Marie along the eastern border of the Lake Superior Provincial Park canoe area, will make canoe pick-ups and drop-offs in

remote areas on request. For further information contact
Algoma Central Passenger Sales
Box 7000
Sault Ste. Marie, Ontario P6A 5P6
Phone 800-461-6822.

The Ontario Northland Railway, which runs from North Bay to Cochrane and Moosonee, will also make pick-ups and drop-offs in remote areas. For further information contact
Ontario Northland
805 Bay Street
Toronto, Ontario M5S 1Y9
Phone 416-965-4268.

Air
For regular scheduled flights by the major airlines see your local travel agent. For an up-to-date list of smaller airlines offering chartered fly-ins to isolated lakes and rivers contact Ontario Travel (address given above) and ask for the free brochure, *Fly-in Services in Ontario.*

Accommodation, Guides and Outfitters
Ontario Travel (address given above) offers a free brochure, *Ontario/Canada Accommodation*, which lists hotels, motels and lodges across the province. The same office offers *Ontario/Canada Camping*, a free brochure listing all private and provincial campgrounds. The same brochure contains a list of outfitters and guides. Outfitters sell food, rent canoes and equipment, and often provide transportation to and from the canoeing area. Guides can add an extra measure of enjoyment and safety to trips, especially on remote, challenging routes or where individuals are uncertain of their canoeing abilities. Services vary considerably according to the guide and may include partial or complete outfitting (equipment rentals and food); custom trips, in which the guide arranges everything in consultation with his client; package trips of varying lengths and degrees of difficulty; and instruction in canoeing skills and outdoor activities. For further information about outfitters and guides contact Ontario Travel, Canoe Ontario or
Ontario Wilderness Guides Association
Box 270
Aurora, Ontario L4G 3H4.

Provincial Parks
General Information
The brochure, *Ontario Provincial Parks*, contains a master list of all provincial parks in Ontario, their locations, services offered and fees charged. It also contains a list of addresses for

all the district offices of the Ministry of Natural Resources, which administer these parks. *Ontario Provincial Parks* and brochures describing individual parks in detail are available free of charge from
The Ministry of Natural Resources
Parks and Recreational Areas Branch
Third Floor, Whitney Block
Queen's Park, Toronto M7A 1W3
Phone 416-965-3081.

Reservations in Provincial Parks
In Algonquin, Killarney and Quetico Provincial Parks daily quotas on the number of people allowed to enter the interiors of the parks have been implemented to minimize over-crowding. For Algonquin and Quetico Parks it is highly recommended that you write well ahead of time to the park itself or to the Parks and Recreational Areas Branch for an Interior Camping Permit Reservation Application. Please specify which park you will be camping in. In all three parks a fee of $3.00 per night, per canoe is charged (at time of writing). This fee includes parking for your vehicle.

Can and Bottle Ban
Cans and glass bottles cannot be used by campers and canoeists in either Algonquin or Quetico Provincial Park. This ban was introduced to promote the use of reusable containers and elimi-nate the litter of broken glass and rusting cans left by careless campers. For details write the Parks and Recreational Areas Branch (address given above).

Hunting and Fishing
Two free brochures, *Summary of Fishing Regulations* and *Summary of Hunting Regulations,* are available from the Parks and Recreational Areas Branch (address given above). For a good description of the kinds and locations of fish and game found in Ontario consult the free brochure, *Ontario/Canada Fishing and Hunting,* available from Ontario Travel (address given above). For information about local hunting and fishing opportunities contact the appropriate district office of the Ministry of Natural Resources.

Topographic Maps
The canoe route brochures you obtain from district offices of the Ministry of Natural Resources and from Conservation Authorities almost always provide a list of recommended topographic maps for each route. These detailed maps are absolutely necessary for navigation. They give information on topographic relief, the location of roads, settlements, rail and power lines, mines, isolated buildings, forest cover, bridges, waterfalls, portages, and the shape and location of lakes and rivers. The knowledgeable canoeist can use these maps to construct a detailed profile of a route before he ever sets eyes on it.

Topographic maps are available in various scales. The scale recommended in each Ministry of Natural Resources or Conservation Authority brochure has been found to be the best for that particular route. When you receive your topographic maps, note the date on which they were published. The older the map the greater the chance that some of its details are no longer quite accurate. For example, a new logging road or power line may have been built.

Topographic maps are available for $2.50 each (this price is subject to change and does not include the 7 per cent sales tax to residents of Ontario) from
The Ministry of Natural Resources
Public Service Centre
Room 1640, Whitney Block
Queen's Park
Toronto, Ontario M7A 1W3
Phone 416-965-6511.

The Public Service Centre also provides, on request, a free index to all topographic maps in Canada.

Some canoeists like to work from aerial photographs, which are available from the Public Service Centre in a wide variety of scales. By piecing a number of these photographs together, canoeists can "see" the lakes and rivers they will be travelling on. Photographs are $2.00 each. (This price is subject to change and does not include the 7 per cent sales tax to residents of Ontario.) The phone number of the Photographs Division is 416-965-1123.

The federal Ministry of Energy, Mines and Resources offers a free brochure, *Maps and Wilderness Canoeing,* which contains an excellent short essay on the reading and use of topographic maps. Write
The Ministry of Energy, Mines and Resources
Canada Map Office
615 Booth Street
Ottawa, Ontario K1A 0E9.

28

Bibliography

Canoeing and Canoe Camping

The number of books about canoeing and canoe camping increases every year. The list below is by no means exhaustive, but it includes a few of the better publications available in bookstores and libraries. The books are listed alphabetically by author.

Cary, Bob. *The Big Wilderness Canoe Manual.* New York: David McKay Co., 1978, 183 pages.

This book is valuable to both beginners and advanced canoeists. It starts with the selection of equipment (the author is not afraid to name brand names) and basic paddle strokes, and progresses to topics such as efficient paddling and low-impact camping. It also contains good sections on packing, family canoeing and fly-in and guided trips.

Davidson, James W. and John Rugge. *The Complete Wilderness Paddler.* New York: Knopf, 1976, 259 pages.

Besides offering a thorough introduction to wilderness canoeing, this book has the advantage of being written in a fluid, anecdotal style. It contains first-rate sections on route planning and tactics—i.e. how to recognize potential difficulties and make the "right" decision.

Evans, G. Heberton. *Canoe Camping: Three.* Cranbury, N.J.: A. S. Barnes, 1977, 186 pages.

This book, well illustrated with photographs, gives sound advice on a wide range of canoe and camping skills, from pitching a tent to camp cookery. The author has led wilderness tours for many years, and his writing bears the stamp of authority and experience.

Franks, C.E.S. *The Canoe and White Water.* Toronto: University of Toronto Press, 1977, 237 pages.

One of the best introductions to rapids running available, this book offers fascinating chapters on the history of the open canoe, whitewater paddle strokes, route planning and much more. *The Canoe and White Water* was written with the rivers of Ontario in mind and should be in every canoeist's library.

Jacobson, Cliff. *Wilderness Canoeing and Camping.* New York: Dutton, 1977, 236 pages.

This book contains a thorough and knowledgeable discussion on a much-debated topic: the selection of the "right" canoe. It also includes excellent designs for spray covers, portage yokes and tumplines, as well as good discussions of trip planning and navigation. There is also a section devoted to trips with children and teenagers. This excellent book is highly recommended to those who wish to start wilderness canoe camping.

Mason, Bill. *Path of the Paddle: An Illustrated Guide to the Art of Canoeing.* Toronto: Van Nostrand Reinhold, 1980, 200 pages.

Superbly illustrated with a selection of exceptionally well-chosen photographs, this book is written by a man whose depth of understanding and love of the world of canoeing will captivate the reader. One of the best books on canoeing techniques ever produced, especially for Canadian waters, this volume is destined to be a classic.

Riviere, Bill. *Pole, Paddle and Portage.* New York: Van Nostrand Reinhold, 1969, 259 pages.

This book, written by a wilderness veteran, makes a good general introduction to canoeing and canoe camping. It has particularly good sections on weather and on poling, an important technique only recently being revived.

Ruck, Wolfgang E. *Canoeing and Kayaking.* Toronto: Coles, 1977, 95 pages.

This is a good short introduction to whitewater canoeing.

Nature Guides

A successful canoe trip involves far more than paddling efficiently from A to B. Many canoeists enrich their travel by expanding their knowledge of the natural world. The following list is by no means exhaustive.

Banfield, A.W.F. *The Mammals of Canada.* Toronto: University of Toronto Press, 1974, 438 pages.

This is a complete reference to mammals in Canada.

Britton, Nathaniel L. and Addison Brown. *An Illustrated Flora of the Northern United States and Canada.* 3 vols. Gloucester, Maine: Peter Smith, 1913. (Paperback reprint, New York: Dover, 1970.)

This comprehensive work is fully illustrated.

Chapman, L.J. and D.F. Putman. *The Physiography of Southern Ontario.* 2nd ed. Toronto: University of Toronto Press, 1973, 386 pages.

Unfortunately, this excellent, detailed work is not matched by any comparable book describing the physiography of northern Ontario.

Courtenay, Booth and James H. Zimmerman. *Wildflowers and Weeds: A Guide in Full Colour.* New York: Van Nostrand Reinhold, 1972, 144 pages.

This is a lavishly illustrated guide to plants of the Great Lakes region.

Fernald, M.L. and A.C. Kinsey. *Edible Wild Plants of Eastern North America.* New York: Harper and Row, 1958, 452 pages.

This is perhaps the best book on the subject of edible plants.

Godfrey, W. Earl. *The Birds of Canada.* Ottawa: National Museum of Canada, 1966, 428 pages.

This is an excellent basic reference work.

The Golden Nature Guides. Racine, Wisconsin: Western Publishing.

These 160-page books, brimming with colour illustrations, make excellent primers. Each book in the series is devoted to a single subject from the natural world.

Holland, W.J. *The Moth Book.* New York: Dover, 1968, 479 pages.

Howe, William H. (ed.) *Butterflies of North America.* New York: Doubleday, 1976, 208 pages.

This book features 2093 butterflies with colour illustrations.

James, R.D., P.L. McLaren and J.C. Barlow. *Annotated Checklist of the Birds of Ontario.* Toronto: Royal Ontario Museum, 1976, 75 pages.

This book lists all the bird species of Ontario and includes information on mating, numbers and distribution.

Judd, W.W. and J. Murray Speirs (eds.) *A Naturalist's Guide to Ontario.* Toronto: University of Toronto Press, 1964, 210 pages.

This book comes highly recommended by professional naturalists.

Klots, Elsie B. *The New Field Book of Freshwater Life.* New York: Putnam, 1966, 398 pages.

This is a guide to all aquatic plants and animals of the United States and Canada.

Logier, E.B.S. *The Snakes of Ontario.* Toronto: University of Toronto Press, 1967, 94 pages.

Mech, L. David. *The Wolf.* New York: Doubleday, 1970, 384 pages.

Miller, Orson K. *Mushrooms of North America.* New York: Dutton, 1972, 360 pages.

This book describes 422 species, with 292 colour photographs.

The Peterson Field Guide Series. Boston: Houghton Mifflin.

The books in this series are excellent for the field identification of birds, animal tracks, trees, wildflowers, butterflies and much more.

Robbins, Chandler, et al. *Birds of North America: A Guide to Field Identification.* Racine, Wisconsin: Western Publishing, 1966, 340 pages.

Scott, W.B. and E.J. Crossman. *Freshwater Fishes of Canada.* Ottawa: Fisheries Research Board, 1973, 966 pages.
This is the basic reference work on Canadian fishes.

Walshe, Shan. *Plants of Quetico.* Toronto: University of Toronto Press, 1980, 216 pages.
Illustrated with more than 200 photographs and written by an experienced naturalist who lives in the North, this guide is useful for most of the Canadian Shield area.

History and Ethnology
It would be impossible to list all the books under this heading that could enrich a canoeist's historical knowledge of an area. The titles included here are only a sampling of the types of writing available.

All travel begins with the canoe itself, so a book like *The Bark Canoes and Skin Boats of North America*, by Edwin Tappan Adney and Howard I. Chapelle (Washington: Smithsonian Institute, 1964, 242 pages) is invaluable as the single most authoritative study of the rich heritage of native peoples' crafts in North America. It illustrates how a variety of canoe designs were used to meet various geographic and climatic conditions. In the same line, Camil Guy's *The Weymontaching Birchbark Canoe* (Ottawa: National Museum of Canada, 1974, 55 pages) is an interesting account of canoe construction by an Indian tribe in Quebec.

Canoeists will also be interested in the Kanawa International Museum of Canoes, Kayaks and Rowing Craft, located thirty-two kilometres north of Minden off Hwy 35. This historical collection includes a wide variety of canoes.

Selwyn Dewdney and Kenneth E. Kidd's *Indian Rock Paintings of the Great Lakes* (Toronto: University of Toronto Press, 2nd ed., 1967, 191 pages) is a pioneering work and still the best introduction to a cultural phenomenon that is well known but little understood.

For the era of European exploration *The Works of Samuel de Champlain*, edited by H.P. Biggar (Toronto: University of Toronto Press, 1971, 6 vols) are a favourite, as are other first-hand accounts, such as those by Alexander Henry, David Thompson and Alexander Mackenzie. *The Fur Trade in Canada*, by Harold Innis (Toronto: University of Toronto Press, rev. ed., 1970, 463 pages) is the best general introduction to the fur trade and its importance to Canada. Eric W. Morse's *Fur Trade Canoe Routes of Canada: Then and Now* (Ottawa: Queen's Printer, 1969, 125 pages) is an excellent history of the voyageurs and the routes they took. Morse has followed all of the main fur-trading routes himself.

There is also a literature written by nineteenth- and twentieth-century recreational canoeists, who combine their own experiences with reflections on the past and on the natural world around them. Many of these books are now out of print and have become collector's items. There are also many reminiscences by old-timers in fur trapping and the lumber trade.

Magazines
The Beaver. This excellent quarterly magazine is read by many people interested in all aspects of Canada's northland. It includes articles on topics such as early exploration, current living conditions, Inuit and Indian cultures and mineral exploration. For information about subscriptions write
Hudson's Bay Company

77 Main Street
Winnipeg, Manitoba R3C 2R1.

Canadian Geographic. This fine magazine comes out six times a year. It often includes articles of interest to canoeists on topics such as hiking and canoeing in wilderness areas, following the routes of early explorers and the present-day state of lakes and rivers. For further information write
Royal Canadian Geographic Society
488 Wilbrod Street
Ottawa, Ontario K1N 6M8.

Films
The National Film Board has produced five short 16-mm films of interest to canoeists. Four are instructional: *Solo Basic, Solo Whitewater, Double Basic* and *Double Whitewater.* These teach basic paddle strokes for flat water and white water. The fifth film, *Song of the Paddle,* follows a family as it canoes the shores of Lake Superior. These films are loaned free of charge by
The National Film Board
1 Lombard Street
Toronto, Ontario M5C 1G6
Phone 416-369-4092.

Other Skills
Department of Indian Affairs and Northern Development. *Northern Survival.* Toronto: Fitzhenry & Whiteside, 1979, 105 pages.
This is an excellent short introduction to emergency survival in northern regions.

Fletcher, Colin. *The Complete Walker.* 2nd ed. New York: Knopf, 1974, 470 pages.
This comprehensive and entertaining book includes much of interest to the thoughtful canoeist, from the choice of packs, camping gear and food to their most efficient use in the wilderness.

Hazen, David. *The Stripper's Guide to Canoe-building.* San Francisco: Tamal Vista Publications, 1976, 96 pages.
This is one of a growing number of books that provide plans and complete directions for those interested in designing and building their own canoes.

Kjellstrom, Bjorn. *Be Expert with Map and Compass.* 2nd ed. New York: Scribner's, 1976, 214 pages.
A guide to the use of maps and compasses, this book contains much of value to the canoeist.

McClane, A.J. (ed.) *McClane's New Standard Fishing Encyclopedia and International Angling Guide.* New York: Holt, Rinehart and Winston, 1974, 1156 pages.
The cornerstone of any good fishing library, this book covers all aspects of technique, equipment and aquatic biology. A classic.

Nourse, Alan E., M.D. *The Outdoorsman's Medical Guide.* New York: Harper and Row, 1974, 135 pages.
Besides teaching basic first aid, this book places special emphasis on temperature-induced problems, such as heat prostration and hypothermia. It also includes good information on topics such as insect bites and the difficulties of treating an injured person in isolated conditions.

Watts, Alan. *Instant Weather Forecasting in Canada.* New York: Dodd, Mead and Co., 1978, 64 pages.
Watts is an author whose writings are esteemed by sailors and outdoorsmen the world over; he equips one with the knowledge to out-forecast the weather office. This book is perhaps best read with an introductory text.

Index